Boundaries
of Dissent

Boundaries of Dissent

Protest and State Power in the Media Age

Bruce D'Arcus

Routledge
Taylor & Francis Group
New York   London

Published in 2006 by
Routledge
Taylor & Francis Group
270 Madison Avenue
New York, NY 10016

Published in Great Britain by
Routledge
Taylor & Francis Group
2 Park Square
Milton Park, Abingdon
Oxon OX14 4RN

Printed in the United States of America on acid-free paper
10 9 8 7 6 5 4 3 2 1

International Standard Book Number-10: 0-415-94872-X (Hardcover) 0-415-94873-8 (Softcover)
International Standard Book Number-13: 978-0-415-94872-2 (Hardcover) 978-0-415-94873-9 (Softcover)
Library of Congress Card Number 2005013429

Library of Congress Cataloging-in-Publication Data

D'Arcus, Bruce.
    Boundaries of dissent : protest and state power in the media age / Bruce D'Arcus.
        p. cm.
    Includes bibliographical references and index.
    ISBN 0-415-94872-X (hb : alk. paper) -- ISBN 0-415-94873-8 (pb : alk. paper)
    1. Protest movements--United States--History--20th century. 2. Protest movements in mass media--History--20th century. 3. Protest movements--United States--Case studies. 4. Mass media--Political aspects--United States--History--20th century. 5. Public spaces--Political aspects--United States--History--20th century. 6. State, The--History--20th century. 7. United States--Politics and government--1945-1989. 8. United States--Politics and government--1989- . 9. United States--Social conditions--1960-1980. 10. United States--Social conditions--1980- . I. Title.

HN59.D38 2005
303.48'4--cd22   2005013429

Taylor & Francis Group
is the Academic Division of Informa plc.

Visit the Taylor & Francis Web site at
http://www.taylorandfrancis.com

and the Routledge Web site at
http://www.routledge-ny.com

Acknowledgments

The work condensed into this book stretches back to graduate school. A lot has happened in the years since, and I've accumulated a lot of debts.

The kernel of this project began life as a dissertation. Don Mitchell was a great advisor: both challenging and supportive. I learned a lot from him and can only hope this work follows his example of politically committed scholarship. My dissertation committee—John Mercer, Mark Monmonier, Beverley Mullings, and Geróid Ó Thauthail—also offered useful feedback that has informed this book.

During the dissertation research, I benefited from funding from both the National Science Foundation and the Syracuse University Geography Department. More recently, Miami University of Ohio has generously supported me with both research and writing grants. The actual research process has been smoothed by the help of archivists and librarians in various places, most notably at the Minnesota State Historical Society in Saint Paul and at the Harvey G. Mudd Library at Princeton.

Nick Blomley has kindly helped me in a few ways, among them his tracking down a copy of the *Tremblay v. Québec* ruling that figures prominently in Chapter 6. Alas, that document is written in French, a language in which I am completely incompetent. I thus consider it good fortune to have run across George Fowler, who helped me out on short notice with an excellent translation of the document.

Colleagues and friends at Syracuse and Miami have provided rewarding diversions as well as productive intellectual exchange; among them are Patricia Ehrkamp, Jim Glassman, Euan Hague, Paul Kingsbury, Nicky Mousset-Jones, Heather Muldoon, Tom Perreault, and Scott Salmon.

My mother and father have always supported my efforts, no matter how odd they may have seemed at the time. More recently, I have spent a lot of time with family in Peru. The list of those I'd like to thank is long, but I would particularly like to thank Emperatriz Velarde, as well as her sisters, Yony and Nina, for their support and good humor as well as their fantastic cooking.

Finally, thanks most of all to Jacqueline, for her love, patience, and companionship.

Portions of this book are revised versions of essays that appeared elsewhere. Parts of Chapter 3, "1968: Drawing the Boundaries of Dissent," appeared as "Dissent, Public Space, and the Politics of Citizenship" in 2004 in *Space & Polity*, 8 (http://www.tandf.co.uk) and as "Protest, Scale and Publicity: The FBI and the *H. Rap Brown Act*" in 2003 in *Antipode*, 35(4); parts of Chapter 4, "Wounded Knee: Native Sovereignty and Media Spectacle," appeared as "Protest, Scale and Publicity: The FBI and the *H. Rap Brown Act*" in 2003 in *Antipode*, 35(4) and as "Contested Boundaries" in 2003 in *Political Geography*, 22(4).

Contents

1

Introduction: Power and Protest in a Media Age

Protest, State Power, and Media Spectacle

In a whole series of events in the past few decades, political protests have placed national identity and state authority in radical question.

Consider three examples separated by time and place. In the 1960s, the Civil Rights movement changed the racial geography of the American South. The legal apartheid of the Jim Crow South tightly regulated who had access to which spaces. Where one could work, where one could eat or drink, and where one could sit on a bus were all structured by the cold logics of what W.E.B. Du Bois metaphorically called the "color line." Yet the color line was more than metaphor and, as much as anything, was about the concrete boundaries that separated people and space. To dismantle this system, activists needed to undo its very logic. To wit, the Civil Rights movement creatively transformed everyday spaces—lunch counters, bus seats, jail cells—into contested political sites.

1

Yet such political spectacles only mattered in the context of a potentially sympathetic audience. In this sense, the Civil Rights movement was not about concrete public spaces alone, but also about access to the larger spatial spheres of mediated symbols. The lunch counter sit-ins that began in Greensboro, NC, were effective in large part because they dramatized that the quasi-public spaces of a restaurant were effectively privatized in the Jim Crow South. The point was made clear to television audiences and news readers throughout the United States and beyond. Likewise, the protests that took place throughout the South were distinguished by their visibility far beyond the specific sites of protest. The centrality of television to the movement was made particularly clear in 1963 in Birmingham, AL, where confrontations between protest marchers and an aggressive police force directed by "Bull" Connor became big news.

Fast forward twenty-something years, to Beijing. Here, in the spring of 1989, Tiananmen Square became the contested public space in which questions of national identity and state authority played out before satellite-connected 24-hour news networks. The Square itself was a geographical and historical crystallization of these dynamics. Long a traditional site of popular and student protests, Tiananmen Square—the largest public space in the world—has also long been an expression of state power. The dual function was crystallized in the monuments to the glory of the state and to the students themselves.

Finally, consider another commonly cited example of an armed uprising in a marginal corner of Mexico. On 1 January 1994, a poorly equipped and trained group of indigenous peasants seized a series of key towns in the state of Chiapas. As Mexican politicians were inaugurating both a new year and a new era of free trade ushered in by NAFTA, the Zapatista movement exploded on the global stage. That the uprising happened on the day NAFTA took effect was no mere coincidence. Zapatista leaders were concerned that the boundary-dissolving drive of the free-trade agreement would put additional pressures on indigenous livelihoods and the lands in which they were rooted. Equally significant, they were concerned about the political process by which Mexico's fate was decided. The seemingly intensely local issue of indigenous land and livelihood was at once also about the place of the nation-state within a wider global arena.

To ensure their concerns were understood within this broader context, the Zapatistas made creative use of the latest communications technologies. They used same technologies associated with the globalization of American consumer culture—the Internet, 24-hour news, and so on—to subvert the relentless march of an emerging McWorld (Barber 1992). As Harry Cleaver argues, "Through their ability to extend their political reach via modern computer networks the Zapatistas and their supporters have woven a new electronic fabric of struggle" that has effectively globalized their efforts and circumvented the Mexican state's attempt to contain the uprising as local and marginal (1998: 81). Such efforts to make the issues articulated by the Zapatistas politically visible, in turn, rested on this movement's ability to speak in terms that were legible to a global public. The struggle of indigenous peasants in rural Mexico, movement spokesperson Subcomandante Marcos made clear, should be understood as a part of a much broader—indeed global—struggle on the part of marginalized peoples for justice and, importantly, dignity. One of the Zapatistas' slogans—"We are here!"—highlighted the importance placed on political visibility tied to identity. The Zapatista uprising thus constituted a situation where, as Stuart Hall has put it more generally, "the margins begin to speak" (1997: 53).

Within this context, geographers have suggested the spatiality of the Zapatista movement goes beyond its use of global media vectors and its articulation of novel connections between identity and space. Paul Routledge, for example, argues that concrete public spaces are of central importance to understanding the movement. "The Zapatistas," he argues, "have attempted to create public space in order to render power visible" (1998: 244). They have done this through a dialectic between the public—visible—spaces of the regional urban centers and the impenetrable shelter of the Lacandon jungle. Their occupation of key public spaces, however, has not been for its own sake, but with the intent of projecting a political statement elsewhere. As Routledge argues, for quite pragmatic reasons the Zapatistas were

> more concerned with the occupation of time on the information network than permanently securing control of Chiapas' major towns. Rather, their material occupation of space was symbolic, staged to gain access to [global] media vectors (1998: 248–49).

To the extent that the Zapatistas have claimed public spaces in the Mexican state of Chiapas as sites of protest, they have also used the de facto private—invisible—spaces of the jungle as sources of refuge and organization. Through this strategy, they were able to turn a marginal corner of Mexico into a highly visible platform for the global public looking on. In turn, the Zapatistas' transient occupations of public spaces in the provinces spread to the heart of the nation, engulfing Mexico City's public spaces in solidarity protests. The Zapatistas are thus a political movement that operates through the manipulation of various kinds of boundaries: between the public spaces of the regional urban centers and the private space of the jungle, between the marginal place of rural Mexico and the central place of Mexico City, and between the domestic concerns of Mexico and the global bonds of solidarity beyond. Indeed, John Ross (2000) has gone so far as to argue that other more recent high-profile anti-globalization protests such as the so-called "Battle in Seattle" could not have happened without the example set by the Zapatistas, as well as the concrete connections they helped forge.

From the lunch counter of a Woolworth's store in North Carolina, to the vast central space of Tiananmen Square in 1989, to the jungles and small-town plazas of Southern Mexico in 1994, activists used the time- and space-collapsing qualities of contemporary media and communications technologies to greatly enhance the visibility of their political claims. By claiming and reworking important public spaces, and doing so before national and even international audiences, contemporary protests occasionally shift relations of power. In turn, states have been prompted to respond in sometimes novel ways to these visibly public expressions of dissent. Such protests thus shed light on the larger geographical dynamics of nation-states; the micro-geographies of the immediate settings of protests bound up in larger scale networks of sympathy and power.

Larger Concerns

In this book, I focus on incidents that place national identity and state authority in radical question. At one level, I present a general examination of the politics of political dissent and state power in the media age. At another, I examine these dynamics through a specifically geographic lens. I am concerned, that is, with how contemporary protest can be understood as a fundamentally geographic praxis.

Although this book deals with social movements, then, it is not about social movements per se. Rather, it is about how movements become public through the political spectacle of protest. Likewise, as much as this book analyzes acts of resistance, it is also crucially concerned with how such resistance is bound up in larger networks and structures of power. In this sense, I will be at pains to break down the often simple dualisms that all too often pose power and resistance, social movement from state. Instead, I focus on the complex valences of different structures of power. Although I am concerned with general discourses and practices that condition and shape what can be done and said, I am most particularly interested in how the state is implicated in such larger dynamics of power. How do states see public dissent and how do they act to shape the conduct of legitimate dissent? What effect does this have on the politics of citizenship?

Finally, although this book focuses on protest politics, it should be clear that I use this substantive and narrative focus as a lens—among many possible lenses—on broader questions of contemporary power and identity, citizenship and marginality, society and geographic space. Among other things, then, I am also concerned with those events that lie on the other side of the line that distinguishes legitimate protests from illegitimate dissent. Examples are myriad, but they are most commonly labeled "disorders" or "riots." As we will see—and as a long tradition of scholarship has shown—such a designation is rarely innocent or obvious, but rather involves situated and politically charged representations of power, identity, and geographic space. As such, how those lines are drawn and policed in practice offers important insight into the nature of democratic citizenship itself. How do events in public space come to be understood as a protest, or as something else? The discursive and performative orders that distinguish a protest from both a riot and casual gatherings on a street are not matters of fact, but expressions of often complex ideas about the relationship between dissent, order, and democratic practice. Individuals and institutions bring these complex normative orders to their understandings of how bodies mingle in space.

An important concern that cuts across all of these issues is how the relationship among these spaces is symbolically mediated. How does media shuttle meaning back and forth across the public/private divide, and with that intervene in the politics of publicity and privacy? How in turn is that meaning circulated across space, and with what effect on the politics of citizenship?

A Road Map

To analyze the geographic dynamics of power and identity characteristic of contemporary protest, I present four case studies. I limit these studies to North America for reasons both practical and narrative. Each event illuminates different historical, political, and geographical moments that nevertheless share certain commonalities. Taken together, they are meant to tell a larger story of modern power and governmentality. All of the cases I examine lie somewhere on one side or the other of the fuzzy and unstable line that distinguishes legitimate protest from illegitimate dissent. They also deal with how the state manages such political spectacles.

In Chapter 2, I present an argument of how to usefully study these issues. Here I draw on recent developments in political and cultural geography, themselves strongly influenced by interdisciplinary work on cultural politics and political theory. I focus this discussion on two interconnected literatures: that on publicity and public space, and that on geographic scale and boundaries. The first—*publicity*—deals with the social construction of citizenship and how this ties to concrete spaces. Given the centrality of public spaces to political protest—and, in the media age, of the more abstract space of a mediated public sphere—careful analysis of how they come to be, how they are regulated, and the precise nature of their connection to power and dissent is essential. Nevertheless, I argue, it is not sufficient to focus solely on the immediate sites of protest, nor only on the more publicly visible aspects of protest, but also on the role of a variety of other potential practices. Moreover, such analysis needs to be fundamentally spatial in orientation. The literature on boundaries and geographic scale allows for just this more complex and nuanced understanding of how power and dissent is articulated in the contemporary media age.

For the historical narrative and case studies I use to make this argument, I begin in 1968. My focus in this chapter is the Civil Rights era, a time in which citizenship was being dramatically challenged in a variety of venues, including on city streets. No issue better crystallized how power, identity, and space came together in complex and contentious ways during this time period than the so-called race riots that swept American cities. The question of how different actors understood the broader significance and root causes of the riots is important enough. Even more important, however, is how those assessments shaped the concrete actions of various state officials: the politicians who crafted laws that attempted to criminalize a particular kind of political activity, the government officials charged with implementing those laws, and the military men who drafted plans to ensure domestic tranquility. In turn, critics often conflated these riots with more overtly political statements like the antiwar protests that took place in Chicago. More importantly, the response to these riots and protests both set the ideological terms by which dissent was later measured and created the legal tools by which it was countered.

In Chapter 4, I turn to similar issues, but played out in a very different geographic and political context. Here we move from city streets and congressional hearings to the marginal world of the Pine Ridge Indian reservation to examine one of the most significant examples of American Indian protest in the 20th century. Here in 1973, at the famous historic site of Wounded Knee, American Indian activists began an occupation that ultimately lasted 71 days. The Wounded Knee occupation is significant for a number of reasons. First, it took place at the end of a long period of activism and political protest in the United States and elsewhere that together constituted a significant intervention in the dynamics of publicity and citizenship in democratic societies. Second, it was a relatively early example of a televised protest and what one commentator at the time, writing in *TV Guide*, described as a "test-tube case of confrontation politics and its symbiosis with the media." The occupation was noted for its spectacular symbolic politics, in which activists articulated, in quite dramatic fashion, treaty rights and the sovereignty claims for which they stood on a global media stage.

The Wounded Knee occupation also attracted the intense interest of the federal government and led to one of the most significant deployments of American state power in domestic space in the 20th century. Significantly, however, senior Nixon administration officials hid much of the exact nature of the state force deployed at Wounded Knee from public view. As a relatively early example of a televised protest—and because of the large number of FBI documents available on the event—the Wounded Knee occupation sheds important light on the geographical dynamics of contemporary mass-mediated protest and on how states act in the context of such political spectacles. That a significant political spectacle like Wounded Knee took place in a geographically marginal location also tells us much about the changing nature of political protest in the media age.

In the remaining two case studies, I examine more contemporary incidents. In Chapter 5, we move to Miami to examine an incident that dramatized neither issues of American Indian territorial sovereignty nor the racial and geographic boundaries that delineated the extremes of wealth and poverty in urban America, but rather a set of international geopolitical issues that were at once about the place of the home in that larger world. In late 1999 and early 2000 the U.S. media was gripped by the spectacle of Elián González. At its most basic the case involved an international custody dispute that pitted the child's extended family against his surviving parent: his father. Yet because the father lived in Cuba and his mother died fleeing the country, the case instantly took on the character of geopolitical spectacle. The question of who would have custody of the child—and therefore of *where* he would go, and who would decide—became a highly contentious one. The role of the federal government in enforcing its authority over such questions quickly became the issue. The drama itself focused on the suburban house of Elián's uncle, where the boy stayed for the duration of his time in Miami. The house served as a metaphor for the larger drama, reflected in the protesters arrayed outside who—brandishing Cuban flags and Catholic symbols—vowed to protect Elián and his new home from the outside intrusion of the state and its illegitimate intention to remove the boy and send him back to Cuba. The army of media personnel who covered this spectacle served to turn this drama into one of national, even global, import. The very public spectacle that took place outside the modest suburban home revolved not only around the grand geopolitical demons conjured up by the Miami Cuban population, but also, at the same time, around arguments concerning domesticity. The home also served to mark off the private space of the domestic from the intensely public space of the spectacle outside and pointed to the deeply political, if often masked, nature of that distinction.

In Chapter 6, I discuss recent antiglobalization protests. The antiglobalization movement came into public being in the United States in late November 1999 in Seattle. There, on the occasion of meetings of the World Trade Organization, activists dramatized their dissent over the politics behind the vast abstractions of neoliberal globalization. Yet beyond the complex ideological stakes involved in the protests in Seattle and a variety of places since, there were also issues of concrete tactics. Activists used a variety of contemporary communications technologies—cell phones and the Internet, most notably—to coordinate their efforts to secure access to key public spaces. Likewise, various state institutions also used creative means to bar or to otherwise control access to those same spaces. This chapter thus analyzes these issues in the context of the antiglobalization protests, focusing in particular on how they played out in and around Québec City during the 2001 Summit of the Americas.

The argument I present in the following chapters involves, on one hand, an assessment of the empirical events I am examining. The highly mediated nature of contemporary protest is a significant change in the geographical dynamics of power and authority. Political dissent is now bound up in far larger worlds than had previously been the case, and both activists and representatives of the state need to have a suitably geographical sensitivity to these changes. On the other hand, and perhaps more significantly, I also present a larger theoretical argument about *how* contemporary power and dissent ought to be studied. In this sense, the argument I present in this book is about more than simply protest spectacles, but also about larger issues of democratic citizenship, identity, and state power.

2
Spaces of Dissent: Public Space and the Politics of Boundaries

Walking in the Park

In May of 2003, protests swept through Peru with lightning speed. President Alejandro Toledo had been elected the year before, replacing quasi-dictator Alberto Fujimori, who had fallen from power in 2001 when videos were leaked to the media conclusively demonstrating deep corruption at the highest levels of government.

Toledo had made his mark on Peruvian politics in part by leading massive protests against the corrupt regime and by election promises of democratic reforms. Yet from the beginning, his broadly neoliberal policies had met with stiff resistance, often expressed in dramatic public protests. This time, however, the protests involved a broad segment of Peruvian society. School-teachers and health workers were angered by government salaries slimmed down by austerity measures, and farmers were angered by rising taxes and exorbitant interest rates. Just as importantly, the protests were *everywhere*: in provincial towns and cities with long-running animosities towards Lima, but also in the heart of the capital city itself. In a twist of geographic irony, Lima's centralizing power was also its vulnerability, as protesters began to cut off all roads into and out of the city in late May.

Toledo's response was itself ironic given his democratic pretensions: a declaration of a state of emergency on May 28. The declaration—a tactic the Peruvian state used aggressively in the 1980s and early 1990s to combat terrorism—removed basic civil rights. Police could freely enter homes or detain people without a warrant. The right to privacy was now void; the state could freely cross the boundary that sheltered citizens from unwanted state intrusion. In addition, the declaration removed the right of assembly. Public space was now dramatically less public; public gatherings were illegal.

The state of emergency declaration was meant to open the roads and to quell the protests. Although effective in the former—largely through military muscle—the protests continued. Now added to the list of grievances protesters dramatized in public spaces throughout the country was the state of emergency itself. Calling the government's show-of-force bluff, protesters refused to cede public space to the president's wish for order. And yet, far from the venues of the most intense protests, I take a walk in the local park. Even here I find evidence of these larger dynamics between citizenship, state power, and public space.

The Parque Kennedy in Miraflores is a vibrant public space. Like all public spaces, it has its structures of order: rules about who is allowed where, how they should behave, and so forth. Nevertheless, this space is used by a diverse array of people—young and old, local resident and outsider, rich and poor—for a diverse array of activities. The park serves as a place to stroll, to make out, to read, to eat, to sleep, to transact business, and to evangelize. It is also a place to dance. Every weekend, a small amphitheater serves host to a large group of mostly elderly dancers. They typically dance to the traditional *Criolla* (Creole) music of the Peruvian coast, but also to the music of the Andes. The dance is always something of an event, with the amphitheater packed with enthusiastic dancers and ringed with almost equally enthusiastic spectators.

On this night, however, the amphitheater sits virtually empty and silent. A sign announces that all public performances in the amphitheater are cancelled because they would violate the provisions against assembly that accompanied the declaration of state of emergency roughly a week before. Despite the sign, the next night the dancers return. An impromptu—technically illegal—dance comes together organically when street musicians begin playing in the amphitheater. There is a euphoria in the air that seems to be a function of both the dance and the deliberate subverting of state authority. As quickly as the public gathering comes together, however, it falls apart. The musicians leave despite pleadings from the dancers: perhaps fearing arrest, or perhaps simply bored, or in search of better-paying opportunities elsewhere.

As I approach the amphitheater the following Sunday afternoon, I again hear music. The same musicians from the previous week's impromptu dance are once again performing for an enthusiastic crowd. This time, however, the crowd is larger, and it is daylight. A few minutes later, a tall police officer descends onto the stage and demands that the musicians cease playing and leave the space. The musicians, however, angrily protest and tell the crowd that despite the wishes of *el pueblo* (the people) for the music to continue, the police officer is enforcing the order against public assembly. The crowd responds with jeers for the police officer and encouragement for the musicians. After a few tense moments, a compromise is reached: The officer allows the musicians enough time to collect contributions from the crowd and to play music while doing so, but must leave thereafter. Despite the moment in which state power is confronted with popular resistance, the music ceases, and the space formerly occupied by the musicians is quickly replaced by a sign reminding park users of the ban.

This is but one example of the larger dynamics among state power, citizenship, and public space as they played out in Peru during May and June of 2003. The contest between state authority and antistatist dissent was dramatized in public spaces throughout the country, but also through the strategic control of the connections *between* them. The spatiality of the conflict was thus quite complex and ranged between a diversity of kinds of spaces, tied together across a variety of geographic scales: from the microscale of bodies in the street to the meso-scale of regional economic development within the nation-state, to the global scale of debates about neoliberal globalization. Despite the declaration of the state of emergency by President Toledo, protests continued throughout the country and forced the government to negotiate on the details of state policy under the pressures of neoliberalism. And yet, even if contested, the declaration was successful in stopping the music in the rather tame venue of the Chabuca Granda amphitheater in the Parque Kennedy.

The example highlights a more general point: that the capacity for states to deploy power, and for citizens to resist, varies widely, as does the manner in which such power and resistance is given form. There is, then, an uneven geography of state power and antistatist dissent. Dissent—and the larger practices of citizenship in which it is wrapped up—is performed in a variety of ways, in a variety of spaces, with a variety of resources and pressures. Although there is a tendency to focus on the most publicly visible spaces of dissent, then, there is a need to look beyond to other spaces as well. Similarly, although there is sometimes a tendency among critical academics to "romanticize resistance," as Lila Abu-Lughod (1990) has put it, it is my contention that it is also important to understand how the state works to shape the geopolitical context in which dissent is articulated. In this chapter, I take up these issues to present a theoretical and conceptual framework that will allow us to more thoroughly analyze the complex dynamics of contemporary political dissent in subsequent chapters.

Citizen, Public, Space

Spectacles of dissent—variously referred to as disorders, protests, demonstrations, riots, and so forth—provide a lens on broader geographic dynamics of citizenship. They provide insight not only into the uneven distributions of rights and responsibilities, identity and power, but they do so in part by making spatially manifest often-intense disagreements about the nature of legitimate dissent; of who is allowed to do what, where, with what kind of symbolic and political effect and weight. My focus, then, is on how such incidents can serve to make politically visible otherwise latent tensions about the intersections of state power, citizenship, and geographic space. Put simply, how do spectacles of dissent dramatize relationships among citizens, the public, and the state? How do citizens materialize their dissent in space? How do their expressions of public dissent travel *across* space; how, in other words, are they mediated? Finally, how do states work to actively shape what Paul Routledge (1994) has referred to as the "terrains of resistance" within which dissent is expressed?

To begin to answer these questions, we must begin with the spaces of the city. The city has always represented both the triumphs and the failures—and certainly the challenges—of democratic life. It is the place where diverse ideas and people are both brought together and kept apart. It represents the most extreme concentrations of wealth and poverty, power and marginality. Largely for these reasons, the city is also the engine of significant change and a lens on society itself. Behind this broad backdrop of citizenship and the city, a myriad of venues we collectively call public space occupy a central place. Streets, parks, plazas, and other such spaces are the very media through which democratic citizenship is played out. The changing way these spaces have been used and imagined, as well as regulated, offers important insights into how rights and responsibilities are understood, and with that, democracy itself. For precisely these reasons, the public spaces of the city have often served as the venues for the most intense—and widely visible—spectacles of dissent.

Citizen and Public

1989 was a significant year in the world of politics and in the historical geography of dissent. It was the year of the Tiananmen

Square democratization protests in Beijing and the subsequent violent—and heavily mediated—reassertion of state authority, as well as a wave of similar protests in Eastern Europe. Likewise, 1989 was the year in which one of the most important boundaries of Cold War Europe—the Berlin Wall—tumbled. Amid this context, the publication of the English translation of Jürgen Habermas' *Structural Transformation of the Public Sphere* (1989) helped crystallize a larger reorientation in Anglophone scholarship toward a more complex view of citizenship and the public sphere. Earlier traditions tended to view citizenship as formal political rights granted by the state: the right to vote, to speak freely, to assemble in space and move across it, and so forth. The broader critical turn in the social sciences has shifted from this view to citizenship understood as a set of practices enacted by individuals and groups. In this view, citizenship is not simply formally held, or not, but rather a social practice that brings together complex identity politics and power dynamics.

Habermas provided both a philosophical argument and a historical narrative that charted the changing architecture of the public sphere. For Habermas, the public sphere offered a realm of relative autonomy from the private spheres of the market and the household, and a check on overaggressive state power. As he put it,

> the bourgeois public sphere may be conceived above all as the sphere of people come together as a public; they soon claimed the public sphere regulated from above against the public authorities themselves, to engage them in a debate over the general rules governing relations in the basically privatized but publicly relevant sphere of commodity exchange and social labor (1989: 27).

The modern public sphere thus provided an interactive forum in which individuals could set aside their private differences and interests to deliberate about important matters of wider—public—concern, against the more narrow interests of both state authority and the private economy. For Habermas, then, a vibrant public sphere that allowed for the productive exchange of often-contrary opinion was the measure of democratic citizenship. Where the state intruded too heavily in regulating the conditions of public debate and interaction, or where private market interests had too much influence in the public sphere, democracy suffered.

Habermas' normative argument for a relatively autonomous public sphere was itself wrapped up in his reading of history and of the historical geography of urban Europe. According to this narrative, the modern citizen—and the public through which it was constituted—emerged amid the spaces of the mercantilist cities of early modern Europe. No longer the economic property of feudal masters or the political subject of monarchy, the modern citizen was nominally free and independent, with the capacity of independent judgment. The changing status of labor thus created an important condition for modern citizenship and the public sphere. Likewise, the increasingly elaborate geographies of mercantile capitalism provide the enhanced traffic in ideas and information necessary to the emergence of a literate public. Among those changes was the emergence for the first time of mass media. Inexpensive and widely available sources of news—published in a common language—provided an important medium for the constitution of modern national publics (Anderson 1983).

Habermas thus placed the emergence of the modern public and the public sphere amid a dynamic historical geography of democratic capitalism. The diversity of people and things and ideas that swirled together into the vortexes of these cities provided the material context for the modern public sphere, and print media provided an important medium for the deliberation and debate that characterized it. Yet Habermas also recognized the central importance of other media through which the modern public sphere was given shape. The spaces of city streets, salons, coffeehouses, and so forth also figured in Habermas' narrative and provided the material setting of face-to-face interactions that were also crucial to the debate and communicative interaction central to public life.

If Habermas' historical narrative begins with the emergence of a relatively intact public sphere, it progresses to its gradual erosion—indeed "disintegration"—under modern bureaucratic capitalism and corporate mass media. The boundaries between the public and private have so blurred for Habermas that the public sphere has lost its essential function as a check on private interests of all kind. As he wrote, under such conditions

> the public sphere assumes advertising functions. The more it can be deployed as a vehicle for political and economic propaganda, the more it becomes unpolitical as a whole and pseudo-privatised (1989: 175).

The increasingly mass-mediated character of the public sphere, the heavy influence of private economic interests on that mediated public sphere, and the increasingly clear fact of the degree to which the state itself—as well as politics more broadly—is mediated all provide the evidence for this decline of the public sphere.

As quickly as the translation was published, however, other scholars picked up the argument and either elaborated on it or radically critiqued it. Habermas' notion of the public sphere as a largely unitary realm of open accessibility whose bounds have expanded and contracted over time tended to obscure an important issue: that within the concept of publicity lies a contradiction. Feminist political theorist Nancy Fraser put the matter succinctly when she argued that the "discourse of publicity touting accessibility, rationality, and the suspension of status hierarchies is itself deployed as a strategy of distinction" (1992: 115). In place of a unitary public sphere either expansive or limited, Fraser argued instead for a notion of the public sphere as fundamentally fractured: crosscut by all manner of differences of both identity and power. Rather than think in terms of a singular public sphere, Fraser argued that it was far more productive—both analytically and politically—to consider multiple public spheres, interacting across intense differences and amid complex hierarchies of power. Contra Habermas, then, for Fraser the public sphere was not a taken-for-granted world of rational talk, but enmeshed in a thoroughly cultural politics. Such a cultural politics included the very distinction that defined publicity itself. As she put it,

> there are no naturally given, a priori boundaries here. What will count as a matter of common concern will be decided precisely through discursive contestation (1992: 71).

Fraser's critical intervention in debates about citizenship and the public sphere pointed to a different set of questions from those raised by Habermas. How are diffcrent kinds of publics constituted, through what kinds of material and representational work, in relation to what distributions of power?

Public Space as Medium of Citizenship

The complexities and ironies of citizenship and publicity are tied up in similar issues related to space. Practices of citizenship are at once spatial practices. Isin (2002), for example, traces historical practices of citizenship—of "being political"—and argues cities function as "difference machines" that do not reflect pre-existing identities, but actively create them. As he puts it,

> the city is a difference machine insofar as it is understood as that configuration that is constituted by the dialogical encounter of groups formed and generated imminently in the process of taking up positions, orienting themselves for and against each other, inventing and assembling strategies and technologies, mobilizing various forms of capital, and making claims to that space that is objectified as "the city"(2002: 49).

In this vision, citizenship is differentially distributed to subjects defined via groups; groups that only come into being through encounters in the spaces of the city. The citizen—as that subject invested with full rights—does not exist apart from relations with its others: those less-than-citizens referred to variously as strangers, barbarians, immigrants, the homeless.

Citizenship and the public sphere is thus played out in a myriad of concrete spaces. From courtrooms and prisons, to school classrooms and sports stadiums, to street corners and public parks, citizenship is a practice that takes place in specific locales. If cities function in general as difference machines that assemble identities and invest them with rights, then it is urban public spaces that provide important concrete settings in which citizenship is enacted. Public space provides an essential role in the politics of citizenship precisely because it is *in* public space that difference is both displayed and encountered. Consider, for example, the rituals of public space, both everyday and spectacular, from a stroll in the park to a military parade to a demonstration. These performances are shaped by the normative frameworks that define the boundaries of acceptable behavior in public space. These frameworks are shaped not so much by formal rules, but by collective expectations and evaluations—even imaginations—of other peoples.

Public space, put simply, is a medium of citizenship: a material space and representational forum through which boundaries of citizenship are drawn and redrawn. Public spaces are tangible material locations and contexts, with volume, and form, and texture. They are also settings in which diverse people interact; where difference is both displayed and encountered. Public spaces are thus something like theaters of social life. They are arenas both to see and to be seen. As Sue Ruddick argues,

> representation of public space is deeply implicated in the process of othering: the way in which certain others are represented in public spaces is not simply a byproduct of other structures of inequity; it is deeply constitutive of our sense of community—who is allowed in, who is excluded, and what roles should be ascribed to "insiders" and "outsiders" (1996: 146).

Public space—much like citizenship itself—is less a taken-for-granted fact than a complex social production. It provides a venue through which excluded groups can represent themselves—make themselves politically *visible*—before larger publics. For Don Mitchell,

> public space is a place within which a political movement can stake out the space that allows it to be *seen.* In public space, political organizations can represent themselves to a larger population. By claiming space in public, by creating public spaces, social groups themselves become public (1995: 115).

For Mitchell, it is precisely the bodily materiality of public space that is so crucial to its function as a space for representation. It provides a platform from which to claim rights, organize representation, and project them to larger publics. Public space, he writes, is ideally "an unconstrained space within which political movements can organize and expand into wider arenas" (1995: 115).

While emphasizing the grounded materiality of public space, then, Mitchell's reliance on the phrase "expand into wider arenas" points to the ways that the politics of public space is at once a politics of scale. If public space provides a setting through which the politics of identity and citizenship are constituted, the mediated character of public space links it to the social production of scale as well. For Ruddick, in the same way that public space provides a medium of citizenship, so does scale. As she writes, "[s]cale . . . can become a medium through which identities are constituted; the constitution of a public space at a particular scale can change the scale at which social identities are constructed, enabling groups to draw and redraw the boundaries defining who is included and excluded" (1996: 140–41). The very notion of "insider" and "outsider" is in fact a geographic metaphor (Sibley 1995) that involves a politics of scale. The community of insiders is a bounded space that might be drawn at the scale of a neighborhood, a city, a nation-state, or even larger civilizational identities of the sort that has become fashionable to emphasize after 9/11.

Public Space, Scale, and the Politics of Dissent

Spectacles of dissent of the sort I analyze in this book bring together issues of identity and power. They involve claims to rights and claims to identity. As such, they provide a lens on larger dynamics of citizenship. If we gain insight into the politics of citizenship in part by examining how they are played out through the media of different kinds of spaces, how might such a perspective inform analysis of the politics of dissent? My starting point is that in the same way that studies of identity and citizenship can be opened up by not assuming bounded and stable objects, but rather inquiring into how boundaries of difference and distinction are operationalized in practice and relationally, so too can the study of the geography of dissent be enhanced by studying how different kinds of spaces are bound and unbound in the context of such crises. My analytical entry point is thus a rich and growing scholarship on boundaries, scale, and publicity.

Scale has been a subject of significant interest and debate within geography for the past decade or so. Precisely as economic globalization was reconfiguring the landscape of capital and labor, and the end of the Cold War was accompanied by a significant redrawing of geopolitical boundaries, geographers sought to revamp theories of scale. In place of earlier traditions that viewed scale in idealist terms as simply an interpretive lens or a set of inert spatial containers—local, regional, national, global—this new scholarship on scale argued that scale was a grounded social-production. As Andrew Herod argued,

> scale is, arguably, geography's core-concept, for only through its resolution can we negotiate the boundaries between difference and similarity. It is scale which allows us to differentiate geographical landscapes, to delimit inclusion or exclusion in such social constructions as

home, class, nation, rural, urban, core, and periphery (1991: 82).

Like space itself, scale is not a thing, but rather a social relationship that involves drawing, redrawing, and transgressing various kinds of spatial boundaries. Scale is not simply there, but is actively produced. As Neil Smith put it, "the continual production and reproduction of scale expresses the geographical contest to establish boundaries between different places, locations, and sites of experience" (1992: 64).

From this perspective, then, there is a *politics* of scale. In the same way that there is a representational politics involved in defining the boundaries between public and private (Staeheli 1996), so too is there in defining boundaries across scale: the authentically local or national against the foreign, or the scale of the home against the world beyond (Marston 2004). Likewise, in the same way that the representational politics of the public sphere are grounded in a more concrete set of dynamics in public space, so too are a representational politics of scale grounded in more concrete efforts to either contain or expand the geographies of connection that constitute a given political movement, governmental architecture, or economic network.

Boundaries are thus embedded in complex hierarchies of power. Politics revolve not just around the transgression of *a* boundary, but rather in the reconfiguration of the relationships between different kinds of boundaries. Smith's concept of "jumping scales" operationalizes this perspective on the politics of scale. Within Smith's framework, different actors deploy power by seeking to define—or to transcend—the scope or extent of a set of social relations. Scale is a bounded space; a temporarily frozen set of sociospatial relations. It provides an analytical lens on how different kinds of spaces and spatial relationships provide interacting media through which different agents either press or inhibit significant social change. With respect to the geography of dissent, then, in this book I will be more interested in how the complex boundary politics of scale work in the context of different kinds of spatial media. Certainly the concrete spaces that provide the immediate setting for spectacles of dissent—the streets, plazas, and parks where bodies assemble in space—will provide an important focus, but so too will other kinds of spaces.

Mediated Spaces

The limitations of Habermas' account of the historical development of the public sphere go beyond his conceptual understanding of the relationship between publicity and difference, however, or his reading of history. Picking up where Fraser left off, Staeheli has suggested the problems with dominant social scientific accounts of the public sphere are that they almost entirely miss the inherent spatiality of publicity and of citizenship. First, scholars often assume a thoroughly uncomplicated relationship between the social construction of publicity and privacy, and their mapping to space. From this perspective, the boundaries between public and private are clear and unwavering; public space is simply where public actions take place. Against this, Staeheli argues—following Fraser—that the distinctions between public and private are socially constructed and that there is a *politics* behind the very distinctions. More than this, however, there is no neat correspondence between the content of people's actions and the spaces in which they occur.

A second problem is of representation. In privileging the concrete spaces of bodily interaction—the traditional public space—the problem of difference and representation is simply deferred elsewhere (Barnett 2003). The problem of representation is itself wrapped up in the problem of mediation; that communication does not travel across any space transparently. Although the "end of public space" thesis that flows from Habermas' narrative tends to be drawn in part around the argument that the public sphere is increasingly mediated—and thus that the concrete spaces of bodily interaction have declined in contemporary importance—this occludes two significant points that are as much empirical as they are conceptual or theoretical. First, even the grounded bodily interactions of the material public spaces of the city are mediated interactions, shaped by all manner of discourses about who is to occupy space and how. Second, and conversely, it confuses the medium for the social practice, tending to ascribe an almost ideal quality to print and electronic media that obscures not only the active and creative ways that individuals and groups use different media—one can consider the simple way that activists of all stripes use phone and e-mail communications to organize more grounded political activities—but also the political economy of communications. Communication, put simply, is work. It involves the active organization and transmission of meaning and information across space.

Champions of the "end of public space" thesis would surely point out that the problem with the increasingly mediated public sphere is precisely its political economy; that the "mass" in mass media refers to the very fact of cultural production under multinational capitalism. Perhaps. Yet such a perspective fails to explain history. It fails to explain why, for example, an activist black counter-public sphere emerged in the American South after World War II despite dominant white control of communications media, nor how contemporary antiglobalization activists are able to exploit the very technologies of communication that are associated with globalization itself. On the other hand, it fails to explain the degree to which the state itself is fully mediated.

Research in social movement theory on framing explicitly takes account of the communicative aspects of social movements and of the larger public worlds in which they are projected. Yet my focus is somewhat different from this movement-based one. I am not so much interested in just how dissenting actors rationally frame their dissent, but also in how various meaning-carrying media serve as virtual spaces through which relationships between citizens, publics, and state are constituted. Put differently, how do various actors seek to constitute the public in ways that serve to position their political project as just and legitimate—as "public"—and others as not? More broadly, how do different kinds of spaces become active media through which boundaries between publicity and privacy are drawn in practice, and with that the distinctions of citizenship itself?

In contemporary mass-mediated protests, communications networks provide a particularly important medium of contest. Indeed, arguably every significant protest movement over the past few decades—from the Civil Rights movement of the 1960s, to the Tiananmen Square protests in 1989, to the Zapatista uprising in 1994—have been heavily shaped by communications media. Adams (1996) suggests that in assessing the connections among scale, communications, and politics it useful to distinguish between the "content" of media and the "context," and explores how "subordinated groups reach beyond the boundaries of place through communication media to substantiate their political claims, create openings for new ideas of scale and new scales of connection, and thereby challenge the social hierarchies embedded in pre-existing territorial contexts" (1996: 420). Using the example of the American Civil Rights movement he writes,

> Many observers, including significant portions of the Black community, initially thought that to attack so small a piece of the segregation system as a bus seat or a "White only" stool at a lunch counter could not make a difference. The tactic was effective not because of the territory it claimed, but because news of the cruel response it provoked became emblematic of racial oppression when carried on the media and aroused the sympathy of distance referenced publics (1996: 435).

Both a public bus and a lunch counter were public by virtue of their nominal accessibility to "the public." Yet the Civil Rights movement highlighted that the boundaries that defined such spaces offered highly differential access based on race. By transgressing the racial norms of behavior associated with these spaces, activists challenged not just the specific spaces in question, but an entire social order. Such tactics, Adams shows, were effective to the degree that these spatial statements could be translated elsewhere. Through a strategic geography of protest aimed in large part at securing media attention, activists engaged a larger world of distant publics. Moreover, this was a political movement that engaged in a politics of scale that not only undid the racial logics of local public spaces, but also "produced a lasting change in Southern territorial practices, and a 30-year swing toward federalism" (Adams 1996: 436). Whether a given event is covered, in what venues, before which mediated publics, with what meaning-laden representations, with what influence are all central questions in the way that communications mediates the scale politics of political dissent.

Law and Public Order

More broadly, public spaces dramatize larger social orders. How we behave in public, how we expect others to behave, and how we imagine public space tells us much about our ideas about social order itself. "As a legal entity, a political theory, and a material space," Mitchell argues, "public space is constructed through a dialectic of inclusion and exclusion, order and disorder, rationality and irrationality, violence and peaceful dissent" (1996: 155). More than simply a setting for difference, then, public space is that complexly interwoven setting where the relationship between citizen and state, power and resistance, identity and marginality come together—in particularly visible ways—in and through space. Public space is where legitimate citizens take part in legitimately public activities and, in so doing, reaffirm their relationship to a state that defines those very boundaries: between the legitimate and the illegitimate, the properly public and private.

In this sense, the regulation of public space is bound up in the regulation of the nation-state as a whole. This is particularly apparent when considering the relationship between public space and law. Law is perhaps the most obvious codification of structures of citizenship. It represents a heavily formalized set of codes that determine the boundaries of inclusion in a community and, with it, establishes a hierarchy of rights. Law determines who is allowed to do what, under what conditions, where. Because "law making is power making," as Benjamin put it, it is "an immediate manifestation of violence" (1978: 295). Citing Benjamin, Mitchell argues that "law making . . . may be an immediate manifestation of violence . . . [but it] is *also* a means for dominant interests to avoid violence by maintaining social order and control" (1996: 295). Put differently, power always involves a dialectic between visible and invisible, public and private, latent and active violence. As a crystallization of power, law itself embodies this dialectic.

For Mitchell, there is a fundamental tension in the very notion of public space. Violence "is considered within the law to be fully transgressive of the boundaries of appropriate behavior in public space." Yet the history of public space shows that it is often "only by being violent that excluded groups have . . . forced the liberalization of public space laws" (Mitchell 1996: 156). In crafting the boundaries of acceptable behavior in public space through the medium of law, then, the state also plays a heavy role in defining public space itself.

But as Mitchell explains, this dialectic of violence is itself bound up in a dialectic of scale. If, as he shows, laws always have specific histories and geographies, law is also by definition universalizing: "Law seeks to enact a set of codes that are placeless and timeless, that are, in the name of justice, free from the variability of local contingency" (1996: 172). By definition, law "must be transferable from one context to another." It is, put simply, an abstraction that seeks to regularize the bounds of proper and improper behavior across an expanse of space. In this sense, law is essential to the ongoing production and reproduction of the nation-state.

The geography of law is complex, however, given form and shape through various kinds of boundaries. Although public space, for example, is as much as anything a legal category, enforced through the weight of state power, it in turn is wrapped up in other legal boundaries. Boundaries delineate legal territories at larger scales through the mechanism of jurisdiction. Like all boundaries, though, the boundaries of jurisdiction are simultaneously material, practical, and discursive. As Richard Ford argues,

> Territorial jurisdiction produces political and social identities. Jurisdictions define the identity of the people that

occupy them. The jurisdictional boundary does more than separate territory; it also separates types of people: native from foreign, urbanites from country folk, citizen from alien, slave from free (1999: 844).

Through these boundaries, law thus structures identity itself in the series of categories it ritualizes: citizen vs. alien, criminal vs. law-abiding public, independent citizen vs. object of state intervention. Like scale more broadly, for Ford "territorial jurisdiction . . . is simultaneously a material technology, a built environment, and a discursive intervention" (1999: 855).

At the same time that law involves the constant drawing and redrawing of social boundaries of inclusion and exclusion, so too are these dynamics often explicitly spatial. As Nick Blomley shows (1994), much of the story of the relationship between law and geography can be told by reference to scale and boundaries. Modern law is fundamentally linked to the modern state and to its centralizing and territorializing practices.

> The construction of that which is deemed law thus rests on the definition of a violent world of nonlaw. The inscription of a frontier—which may be figurative, temporal, and spatial—is integral to this process (Blomley 1994: 124).

The territory beyond law is that which is beyond the state. Law is thus a crucial mechanism through which states intervene in the dynamics of dissent and sets the very boundaries by which it is measured. If communications provide one kind of spatial medium through which the politics of dissent are played out, then law provides another.

In entering into this interpretative politics, states also shape the contours of dissent. In general terms, states set the normative boundaries of legitimate dissent and the objects of intervention. Primarily through the mechanism of law, states determine who is invested with what rights, and with that determination intervene in identity itself. Legal discourse and state practice constitute all manner of subjects through these mechanisms: from welfare mothers to immigrants and would-be terrorists, to prostitutes and the homeless. Most fundamentally, then, in the management of conduct, state practices specify the contours of who is allowed to do what, where.

Reading the Riot

This book examines relationships between public dissent and state power, and draws on a larger body of scholarship about power and resistance, identity and otherness, law and disorder, citizenship and marginality (Brown 1997; Hubbard 2001; Mitchell 2003a; Sharp et al. 2000). Although there is a rich body of scholarship on the complex spatial dynamics of protest politics as resistance (Adams 1996; Miller 2000; Routledge 1994, 2003), less thoroughly studied—or theorized—is the view not from resistant groups challenging authority through their occupation of space, but rather from the authority that views such occupations as illegitimate [1]. As part of a broader pattern of "contentious politics" (Martin and Miller 2003; McAdam, Tarrow, and Tilly 2001), riots present often radical challenges not only to state-imposed authority, but also to state-centered discursive orders. As such, they can provide a lens on larger structures of citizenship.

Riots are one kind of dissent in public space, with an important place in the history of social change and in the development of the modern state. Riots have typically challenged state-imposed order, either by directly defying state authority—as in, say, the 19th century draft riots in the United States (Headley 1873)—or by providing alternative normative orders of the sort that E. P. Thompson famously discussed (1971), and often in serving as vigilante justice of sorts (Gilje 1996). Riots are, in short and by definition, beyond the law. As such, riots also have a long place in legal tradition. In such tradition, riots were in essence what officials of the state claimed them to be. One riot act from 1771 Pennsylvania described a riot as

> any persons, to the number of twelve, or more, . . . unlawfully, riotously, and tumultuously assembled together, to

the disturbance of the public peace (*An act for preventing tumults and riotous assemblies* 1771).

On the occasion of such disturbances, a representative of the state was dispatched to the scene to read the riot act, in excruciating detail. Once complete, all of those within the immediate area had an hour to return to the private spaces of their homes. In essence, the state temporarily removed the most basic of liberal citizenship rights—that of assembly—from an expanse of (typically urban) space.

In an era of protest permits and mass-mediated curfew declarations, the practice of reading the riot act seems rather arcane. Yet the practice of withholding rights to particular public spaces in particular times in the interest of preserving state-imposed order is still with us. So too are the *politics* of riots. What precisely constitutes a riot is often in the eye of the beholder and wrapped up in larger identity politics. Writing in the late 1950s, for example, George Rudé argued that the most typical English usage of the word "mob" was as a generic term that applied to crowds engaged in a wide range of activities—from strikes to political protests—who were typically "frequently assumed, without further investigation, to be the passive instruments of outside parties and to have no particular motives of their own other than loot, lucre, free drinks, or the satisfaction of some lurking criminal instinct" (1959: 1–2). For Rudé such interpretations symbolically denied citizenship to those disrupting norms of public order by virtue of their presumed inability to maintain the bounded and self-interested behavior of the proper citizen. Action was not intentional and reflective, but rather impulsive and guided by outside interests, thus rendering it illegitimate. Discourses of community, scale, and citizenship thus intersected in hegemonic readings of public dissent.

A generation of scholars has followed Rudé in challenging this perspective, arguing that riots and other disorderly public events are neither particularly unique nor inscrutable. Instead, they reveal the complexities of power and identity, citizenship and marginality, law and (dis)order. In so doing, they offer insight into social and historical change more broadly. The interpretive politics that distinguish a riot from a protest from a gathering on the street are seldom clear or uncontested. Even where there is broad agreement that a given event is, in fact, a riot, there may be vastly diverging interpretations of the meaning of the event in question. Indeed, the events to which the colonial antiriot act was designed to respond were subsequently interpreted by historians and others as the beginnings of the American Revolution.

Riots are perplexing in large measure because they upset standard norms about the practice of dissent in public space. As one study of reactions to the riots of the 1960s put it,

> the riots were not orderly gatherings that proceeded during the daytime along fixed and highly visible routes selected well in advance. To the contrary, they were without leaders and outside the law. The rioters did not march past a single spot or assemble in a special place; nor did they identify themselves to newsmen or sign their names to public statements (Hill and Folgelson 1969: 6).

Riots are thus events that take place in public space, but which conform to none of the ordered logics of the more acceptable performance of a protest. For critics, riots typically are in part illegitimate because they make no political sense. They appear random and without logic. Yet this assessment of political and moral legitimacy is itself conditioned on a spatial interpretation. Protests are spatially concentrated. They establish a clear demarcation in space—one unlikely to be breached—between those performing dissent and those observing the spectacle from a distance, whether public bystanders or prime-time television viewers. To the degree that a protest march moves *through* space, it is along a clearly defined path: one set out beforehand, and thus without surprise. Finally, the legitimate protest takes place before the clarifying light of day, where all the ordered ritual of its performance could be clearly seen by all.

Contrast this with the riot, where bodies are diffuse in space, where their movement *through* space is unpredictable and potentially chaotic, where there exists no movement leader to articulate a legible political statement before a larger public, and where the confusion and ambiguity of it all is greatly enhanced by the fact that the spectacle generally occurs at night [2].

Public unrest like riots also presents challenges for social scientific explanation. In his work on the Zoot Suit Riots that took place in Los Angeles in 1943, Eduardo Obregón Pagán (2000) argues that scholars all too frequently rely on general historical explanations—that, for example, the violence was a product of pervasive white racism, fanned by sensational news accounts—and in the process miss more complex spatial explanations. Instead he shows that the conflict emerged out of quite grounded encounters in public space that brought together race, class, and masculinity in tense ways. Similarly, Marilynn Johnson (1998) argues that research on riots is burdened by limitations around gender that are both conceptual and methodological. In the first, scholars often assume that the active agent of riot violence is male, and that women typically do not participate. Methodologically, historical research often relies on arrest records as a proxy for active riot participation. However, arrest records themselves reflect the biases of the officers.

Riots are thus political spectacles that periodically open up crises of representation. They commonly elicit contentious debates about the nature of political representation. Citizenship—as either normative right or abdicated responsibility—is presented for critical scrutiny before the glare of the public spotlight. Secondly, and consequently, the crisis of political representation—in essence, of who state power serves, and who it victimizes—is also inseparable from a crisis of symbol: namely of how to discursively order such spectacles, events that are interpreted as both beyond the law and beyond the bounds of normality that allow for easy sense-making and truth claims.

Such episodes—and in particular how they are interpreted and in turn managed—are useful diagnostics of power (Cresswell 2000). They can tell us much about the existing contours of citizenship, of who has the power to do what, to represent truth in what ways, with respect to what kinds of distributions of identity and subjectivity. Riots are a useful lens on citizenship precisely as they represent in some sense the breakdown of citizenship. They are also useful lenses on the *geography* of citizenship because these issues are always articulated spatially. The unsettled boundaries of dissent that accompany interpretation of riots and other such episodes of public dissent reveal how those boundaries—including a variety of geographic boundaries—are otherwise ritualized in everyday practice.

Conclusions

Spectacles of dissent—protests, demonstrations, riots, and so forth—bring together citizenship, law, and public space in complex and dynamic ways. My question is less about why particular spectacles of dissent happen than about how different actors marshal various kinds of resources to press their claims in and through space. Public space provides the most concrete and bodily medium of dissent. However, in the same way that we need to avoid black-boxing who and what is public, we also need to avoid taking for granted that the concrete geographic settings of public space are the only meaningful analytical entry point for studies of protest. Indeed, my argument in this book is that a narrow focus on simply the publicly visible manifestations of dissent as they take place in public space is increasingly limiting in today's protest landscape[3]. To put this differently, we need to consider exactly what public space *is* in the contemporary satellite-connected, Internet-enabled, globalized world in which we now live.

Although urban public spaces have been and continue to be the primary geographic venue of protest politics, it is hard not to recognize the degree to which the dynamics of protest have spilled far beyond the boundaries of the city. On one hand, examples like the Zapatista movement show that high-profile political spectacles can take place in locations far removed from urban public spaces. The instantaneous communications of CNN and the Internet greatly expands the geographic realm in which protest events can potentially insert themselves. On the other hand, protesters frequently travel great distances, across international boundaries even, to access specific protest sites. There is thus a dual sense in which the geographies of contemporary protest politics have changed.

The past decade has witnessed renewed interest in boundaries across the social sciences and humanities. In part, they represent a metaphor for something else: the nature of identity, the distributions of power, the distinctions of citizenship. Boundaries as deployed in the context of contemporary critical social theory provide a conceptual language to talk about all of these issues in more flexible and dynamic ways than other metaphors of territory or place or space. They call attention not to the content of objects, but to the edges that define them.

I advocate here a focus on boundaries, however, that is rather more broad than the largely linguistic focus of poststructuralist literary theory and philosophy. Boundaries are both discourses as well as tangible material things that divide people and things in ways both violent and nurturing, constraining and enabling, spectacular and mundane (Kirby 1996). The framework I present in this book focuses on dissent as a fundamentally spatial practice. Rather than simply asserting yet again the importance of a geographic perspective, however, I use an analytical focus on boundaries and scale to critically analyze *how* a spatial perspective sheds important light on the dynamics of contemporary protest, and with it the nature of democratic citizenship itself. Of necessity, then, it also means carefully avoiding—to the degree possible—fetishizing space as an object with an inert and autonomous existence. Space is but one aspect of social life more broadly. As such, in the following chapters, I adopt a largely antidisciplinary perspective, drawing on the innovations not only in geographic theory, but also in cultural and political theory, as well as social history.

Spaces of dissent are one media through which citizenship is constituted. Bringing together theories of public space with theories of boundaries and geographic scale can offer a more nuanced understanding of both the geography and the politics of dissent. Likewise, conceiving of public space less as just a thing than as a

networked web of intersecting spaces and spatial relationships—from the normalizing space of the law to the symbolic
spaces of different kinds of communications media to the roads
and highways that move people and things across space—can
provide richer insight into how power is both normalized and
contested. Although I am thus interested in offering a more complex view of the spatiality of dissent, I am also interested in a
more complex view of the *politics* of dissent.

Indeed, American political history has often hinged on the
intersections of scale, law, and citizenship. In the early republic,
both the Federalists and the Anti-Federalists, Blomley argues,
had quite clear—and irreconcilable—perspectives on the relationship between the local and the national as they intersected in
the state. For the Federalists, the local was the site of narrow and
particular interests, and the setting most likely to be dominated
by entrenched, antidemocratic elites. For the Anti-Federalists, by
contrast, the local was the site of authentic democratic practice.
"Localized political life," Blomley writes of this vision, "was now
recast as virtuous and ontologically necessary" (1994: 118). The
federalizing state was thus, for the Anti-Federalists, threatening
to the very principles of democratic life understood fundamentally as embedded in the local.

This political calculus of scale runs throughout American history. As the next chapter suggests, perhaps at no time was this
more explicit than in the 1960s, as questions of race and citizenship were cast with explicit reference to geographies of scale and
boundaries. When conservatives argued for "states' rights" they
did so to blunt social change in local places so as to preserve what
they regarded as their organic character. That character, in turn,
was defined with reference to a public—a "Silent Majority"—that
had not been public enough. In the next chapter, we examine
how various actors shaped the dynamics of citizenship and scale
in the late 1960s.

3

1968: Drawing the Boundaries of Dissent

The streets are yours. Take 'em.

> — H. Rap Brown (in U.S. Senate 1967a: 33)

[M]en must fear the law to respect it. The Good Book says that the fear of God is the beginning of wisdom, and the fear of the law is the beginning of good behavior.

> — T. W. Davidson, lawyer from Houston
> (in U.S. Senate 1967a: 9)

1968 was a momentous year in the history of contemporary political dissent. Significant public spaces around the world became the contested sites in which questions of power and identity played out before national and international audiences. These confrontations pitted protesters—often students—against the cold machinery of the state: police officers, military troops, tanks.

In May, the public spaces of Paris became the stages on which activists dramatized issues of alienation and marginalization. The movement began with students at Naterre University protesting conditions there, but quickly drew in students from the Sorbonne as well. University administrators responded to the crisis by calling in the security forces, which only served to heighten the tensions. The conflict culminated in the "Night of the Barricades," where activists closed off sections of the medieval Latin Quarter by sealing its narrow and winding streets with barricades. Just as the revolutionaries of the Paris Commune had done nearly a century earlier, protesters asserted their rights to French society by asserting their rights to city spaces. On the other side of Cold War geopolitical Europe, activists called for democratic reforms in Prague. Again, significant public spaces, such as Wenceslaus Square, became the sites in which dissenters dramatized their concerns.

And then . . . Chicago. The events as they came together on the streets of Chicago began long before the Democratic Convention. Activists from around the country had been planning massive demonstrations for months. Organizers had traveled across the country to solicit support for the antiwar protest. For activists, Chicago was the stage to dramatize antiwar dissent. In late July, organizers applied for permits for two demonstrations: one a march to Grant Park, and the other from there to the Chicago Amphitheater, which would be the site of a massive rally. In addition, organizers also requested permission to use various city parks—among them Grant and Lincoln Park—as places to sleep and to assemble more informally. In short, protest organizers insisted on both broad access to city public spaces, as well as specific access to the protest platform of the amphitheater. Although they recognized potential difficulties with their demands on the city's public spaces—their planned march through the streets would, for example, thread its way through black and working-class neighborhoods that might not take kindly to the intrusion of middle-class white protesters and large numbers of police officers—they still believed that the political stakes were too high to cede strategic spaces to the ordered status quo.

Chicago Mayor Richard Daley could not have held a more contrary view of the meaning of the city and its public spaces. Daley privileged order above all else. He articulated this perspective in public statements such as, "No one is going to take over the city. ... We'll permit them to act as American citizens and in no other way" (in Farber 1988: 122). It was also reflected in concrete decisions by Daley and his deputies. They effectively rejected, for example, all of the permits requested by the protest organizers, citing security concerns among others.

The conflicting perspectives came to a head in particular over access to two parks: Lincoln Park and Grant Park. Officials in part rejected the permit to sleep in Grant Park because they felt it would sully what the Deputy Mayor called the "city's living room" (Epstein 1970: 198). The metaphor seems particularly telling: a space both central and for display, but also a private space for a bounded community. Despite their lack of permits, activists assembled in the park anyway, with people like Tom Hayden declaring that "Lincoln Park is our territory" (in Farber 1988: 175). The first night, Chicago Police Commander Robert Lynsky ordered his officers to aggressively clear the park, believing that not doing so "would be interpreted by the demonstrators as signs of weakness and would only lead to further confrontation" (in Farber 1988: 174). The police cleared the park without serious incident, but the next day similar tensions exploded in Grant Park. The incident began a period of violent conflict between protesters and police, which was dramatized in the media.

The conflict over the right to dissent in Chicago was a familiar one that had played out in myriad locations in the previous years. On one side were advocates of social change who made their claims in and through public space. The whole point, of course, was to upend the everyday orders of public space, and with it society itself. Disorder was a necessary tactic to a greater purpose. On the other side were those suspicious of or hostile to the disruptions that such public dissent implied. To allow dissent was by definition to allow disruption of everyday order and to open up the possibility of anarchy.

Yet if the conflicts at issue in Chicago reflected long-standing tensions over citizenship and dissent in a democratic society, there were two factors that made Chicago somewhat unique. First, the police charged with enforcing local state authority did so with massive, almost theatrical, violence. Not only were the protesters beaten—sometimes viciously—but so too were innocent bystanders, including news reporters. All of this opened up interpretive questions of exactly what to name the events in question. Was it a protest? A demonstration-cum-riot enacted by what Daley referred to as "a lawless violent group of terrorists" (in Farber 1988: 203)? Or was this instead an event that suggested a vastly different understanding of the causal agents behind public violence; a "police riot"?

The second, and closely related, factor that made Chicago unique was the intensely mediated nature of the events. If it was hyperbole to suggest that the whole world really was watching the events that took place on the streets of Chicago—as protesters chanted to television cameras—virtually everything *was* captured by network news cameras and broadcast on evening news programs. In a way not unlike the impact of prime-time news footage of Vietnam on public opinion about the meaning of otherwise distant violence, the coverage of Chicago greatly enhanced the profile of the event and lent it an immediacy that made the issues all the more intensely felt.

In some sense, 1968 marked a turning point in which protest became global. A common experience of consumerism, bureaucratization, and Cold War militarism helped create the concrete conditions for significant protest movements with common goals. At the same time, the new world of television news linked these protests in symbolic terms as well. Yet although there was much that linked these protests across national boundaries, it was also the case that they were particularized by their place within a world carved up by nation-states. As much as many protests shared a common set of symbols and concerns, they also took place within unique contexts of national identity and state power. In this chapter, I situate my discussion by focusing on how various actors intervened in the dynamics of publicity, scale, and protest in 1968. I do this by analyzing how public debate about the meaning and significance of urban unrest—incidents referred to variably as protests or riots, depending on the political ground on which one stood—was expressed in state policy. In particular, I examine the historical geography of the Federal *Anti-riot Act*. The law emerged as a response to ghetto riots spurred by what its sponsors conceived of as deviant black men, but which government prosecutors first used to prosecute high-profile and mostly white New Left activists in Chicago, and later—as we will see in Chapter 4—most extensively used to manage a crisis in a space quite far removed from the city spaces for which its authors originally designed it.

Riots, Citizenship, and the City: J. Edgar Hoover and the Rabble-Rousers

The events of Chicago must be placed in larger context. American cities, according to Monkkonnen (1981: 539), have historically been characterized "as violent, noisy, chaotic, and disorderly." Such notions of disorder, he further points out, have in turn been linked to understandings of specifically *urban* public spaces; *urban* because cities "are characterized by relatively intensive use of public space by people of all classes," and *public* because it is only *in* public that such disorder is made *visible*—as he says "open to observation"—*by* the public. But if there is a general history of viewing the city as a site of disorder, there is a more specific history, and indeed geography, by which particular cities are understood in specific times as disorderly in specific ways. The re-emergence of the city as a site (and sign) of disorder in the 1960s was particularly intense. Yet it also took on a particular form, however, in which unrest in particular cities was understood by many to be symptomatic of a larger *national* problem. In turn, this national problem also raised concerns about a larger, and more sinister, geopolitical problem.

In the Civil Rights era, activists dramatically challenged the politics of American citizenship in a variety of venues, including on city streets. No issue better crystallized how power, identity, and space came together in complex and contentious ways during this time period than the so-called race riots that swept American cities. In 1967 alone, the Kerner Commission—charged by President Johnson with studying the riots—found 164 "disorders," eight of which they classified as "major," characterized by

1. Many fires, intensive looting, and reports of sniping
2. Violence lasting more than 2 days
3. Sizeable crowds
4. Use of National Guard or federal forces as well as other control forces (National Advisory Commission on Civil Disorders 1968: 113)

The Commission classified an additional 33 incidents as "serious." In short, the Commission found that roughly 25 percent of disorders reported in the first 9 months of 1967 were severe enough to categorize as riots. According to a Senate subcommittee, the riots resulted in a reported 83 deaths and 1897 injuries. Damage estimates in the most severe riots initially ranged as high as $25 million in Detroit and $500 million in Newark and only later dropped to $10.2 million and $45 million, respectively (National Advisory Commission on Civil Disorders 1968: 115).

With respect to the geography of the disorders, the Commission found that the majority of the most severe disorders were limited to major urban centers—though not with any particular regional pattern—and localized for the most part in black ghettoes. The Commission found the riots to have emerged in most cases amid what it referred to as "an increasingly disturbed social atmosphere, in which typically a series of tension-heightening incidents over a period of weeks or months became linked in the minds of many in the Negro community with a reservoir of underlying grievances" (National Advisory Commission on Civil Disorders 1968: 6). This "reservoir of grievances" included unemployment and poor housing tied to a reorganization of the economic geography of capital and the social geography of race and class: the in-migration of poor blacks—many of them migrants from the South—into inner-cities, and the out-migration of whites and middle-class blacks, as well as capital. Yet the most serious grievances the Commission identified—and the most frequent catalysts of unrest—were policing practices. Indeed, the Commission cited otherwise routine encounters between police and black residents as the most common proximate cause of riots.

The Kerner Commission's conclusions were controversial and were hardly the only word on the riots. In 1968, these riots were a common topic of discussion in American magazines, newspapers, and television shows, as was the status of the nation's cities. The sheer volume of coverage of this issue in news reporting, commentary, and letters to editor suggests that, as a phenomenon that was taken to represent a larger national problem or threat, the riot as a marker of urban disorder was troubling for many [4].

The interpretive politics surrounding the riots were staked out around a variety of metaphors. Some commentators, for example, drew comparisons between the riots and carnival, in which a catharsis accompanied the upending of everyday life. In surveying the damage of a major riot that hit Detroit in 1967, Mayor Jerome Cavanagh characterized participants in the riots there as "filled with a carnival spirit. … Rioting has become a lark, a joke. There's a sense of euphoria in the air" (*Newsweek* 1967a: 19). Much of what *Newsweek* referred to as the "carnival gaiety" of the riots revolved around looting, which involves the transgression of a number of boundaries, spatial and otherwise. The most basic transgression involved ownership itself. Marx's notion of the "fetish of the commodity"—in which objects are invested with an independent existence and character—itself is a spatial relationship. Store windows separate the pedestrian on the street from the object of intended desire inside. Looting, as the Situationists argued in response to the Watts riots (*Situationists International* 1965), literally shatters that spatial relationship and the social fictions they argued structure it.

Others argued not that the world of civilization was turned upside down in the carnivalesque riot, but rather that civilization was completely evacuated from ghetto spaces. In touring the devastation of Newark, for example, New Jersey Governor Richard Hughes argued that "[t]he line between the jungle and the law might as well be drawn here as anywhere in America" (*Newsweek* 1967b: 22). In their rhetoric, law-and-order politicians and citizens constructed ghetto spaces as, on one hand, largely passive victims of outside forces. On the other hand, politicians and other public figures rendered the passivity of the ghetto before the onslaught of these outside forces as a function of a socially and morally bankrupt subject population. Ghetto residents were seen here as capable of managing neither their own conduct nor that of others. Citizenship thus became a responsibility abdicated, by force of either will or nature. Law-and-order politics thus located responsibility for the riots in a variety of sources, from communist and other Left ideologies to federal government programs designed to ameliorate ghetto conditions. Yet they invested no figure with as much causal significance as the "outside agitator."

The concern about urban riots led many—politicians, academics, the public (or more precisely, *a* public)—to demand answers. The question of how different actors understood the broader significance and root causes of the riots is important enough. Even more important, however, is how those assessments shaped the concrete actions of various state officials: the politicians who crafted laws that attempted to criminalize a particular kind of political activity, and the government officials charged with implementing those laws. In response to broad concern about riots, President Johnson established a National Advisory Commission on Civil Disorders, whose task was both to understand the "origins of the recent major civil disorders in our cities" and, more importantly, to make recommendations on "methods and techniques of averting or controlling such disorders" in the future (U.S. Senate Select Committee to Study Governmental Operations with Respect to Intelligence Activities 1976: 491).

To this end, FBI Director J. Edgar Hoover appeared before the Commission to discuss the role of a new kind of radical in these disorders: what he referred to as "rabble-rousers." As Hoover argued to the Commission, these individuals represented a new, highly mobile threat. By taking advantage of contemporary communications and transportation technologies, these rabble-rousers—who, as he put it, "initiate action and then disappear"—were largely responsible for the unrest plaguing American cities. To keep close tabs on just such "subversives," Hoover had established the Rabble-Rouser Index in 1967, a list that specified who these people were and where they lived. Hoover understood these subversives in explicitly racial terms: as "racial agitators and individuals who have demonstrated a propensity for fomenting racial discord" (U.S. Senate Select Committee to Study Governmental Operations with Respect to Intelligence Activities 1976: 511). The politics of race also encompassed a politics of space and scale, as FBI instructions specified that "only individuals . . . of national interest be included on this index." And "[p]articular consideration," instructions continued, "should be given to . . . those . . . who travel extensively." From this perspective, Hoover placed the problem of the nation's cities at the foot of a new kind of individual: mobile and unattached to particular locales, these outsiders freely moved across state boundaries, stirring up trouble where it had not previously been. Like the public bandits of the Depression years, Hoover again resurrected the mobile criminal as necessitating state intervention in the interest of protecting the public [5].

The "Outside Agitator" and the Duties of Citizenship

Hoover's perspective reflected a broader understanding of the changing political geography of dissent in the United States. In this section, I explore how various government officials made sense of the crisis of citizenship presented by the "race riots" that wracked American cities and with this crisis set the ground for particular kinds of government intervention. Although this is a rather broad subject, I focus on one particular aspect here: namely, how conservative politicians worked to place responsibility for the riots in the hands of a conspiracy of individuals, constructed as both deviant black men, but also as criminal outsiders.

Moreover, I argue, in doing so, those articulating this law-and-order rhetoric made arguments about the status of both the ghettoes and the citizens who inhabited them.

The arguments presented by law-and-order critics hinged on notions of citizenship, law, and public space. Here public space—and by extension society itself—was normatively envisioned as safe and orderly. As one political pamphlet entitled *In Support of the Law and an Orderly Government* put the matter:

> Under the guise of Right of Assembly minority groups have been permitted to assemble on public streets to block traffic, at entrances to buildings to prevent entrance of others, and to disrupt whole communities with total disregard for the rights of others (*Congressional Record* 1968: 9181).

In this interpretation, the rights of citizens were being trampled by a variety of less-than-citizens who were turning public spaces into spaces of danger and chaos.

As they sought to respond to this crisis of citizenship and of government, conservative politicians relied on similar notions of order and public space. One of the more vocal Southern law-and-order Democrats was Robert Byrd of West Virginia. On the occasion of unrest associated with the 1968 sanitation workers strike in Memphis, Byrd interpreted Martin Luther King's role in the following way:

> Martin Luther King fled the scene. He took to his heels and disappeared, leaving it to others to cope with the destructive forces he had helped to unleash. And I hope that well-meaning Negro leaders and individuals in the Negro community in Washington will now take a new look at this man who gets other people into trouble, and then takes off like a scared rabbit (Byrd 2004).

For Byrd, citizenship involved the responsible conduct of one's own behavior in conformance with the rule of law. King violated the duties of citizenship both by transgressing the bounds of acceptable behavior in public space, but also by geographically avoiding the consequences of such a transgression. This is the essence of the outside agitator argument: that individual inciters enter localities from elsewhere, spark unrest that otherwise would not occur, and then disappear, leaving local communities to deal with the aftermath.

In the more formal venue of a student newspaper editorial, Byrd had earlier offered a more comprehensive perspective on the politics of public dissent (1967), attempting in the process to make sense of a contradiction. On one hand, various law enforcement officials had argued strongly for the outside agitator thesis. On the other, prominent officials such as Hoover himself had argued the riots were spontaneous events without significant outside influence. Byrd sought to split the difference by arguing a more subtle outside influence. The cause-and-effect relationship for Byrd was not a direct one of bodies in space, but rather a larger context shaped by the circulation of ideas and images. Byrd cited as influences a variety of essentially moral failings of society: the decline of family and public religion, the tolerance of criminality, and a decadent culture. All of these influences provided the context of tolerance that allowed and even encouraged transgressions of law as evidenced in the riots.

Yet Byrd also went on to "especially cite," as he put it, another factor that did explicitly link the outside agitators to the ghetto riots: the influence of the media in granting them "unwarranted publicity" that both amplified their words and circulated them across space, investing them with causal force. "The incredible over-emphasis given these new revolutionaries in the news has carried their influence—distorted beyond proper proportion—into the remotest corners of the land" (Byrd 1967). Whether Byrd argued the indirect media-based perspective, or the more direct bodily perspective he used to critique King, the ultimate argument was the same: that public unrest in place was a product of outside influence, and thus illegitimate.

Byrd was prominent in Congressional debate on the subject of political dissent and frequently introduced commentary into the record, both by himself, as in the editorial example above, and by others with whom he sympathized. One such piece of opinion was delivered in a speech before the West Virginia State Bar Association by then-president William C. Beatty. Beginning with the assertion that "the greatest current threat to free expression in the country is the so-called doctrine of civil disobedience" (1967), Beatty went on to discuss the connection between democratic rights of speech and assembly in public space on the one hand, and order on the other. First, he argued, the moral boundaries of law were absolute and clear. The notion—central to the Civil Rights movement—that unjust laws ought to be transgressed was thus illegitimate. Second, Beatty connected this to an argument about assembly and speech. As he put it,

> Civil disobedience is neither non-violent nor peaceful. Massing and marching and blocking streets from intended use is not peaceful assembly. Interfering with the function of public universities is not academic freedom, nor is the use of despicable four letter words by bearded youth in public gatherings. Trespass and destruction of property is certainly not freedom of expression. But all of these things are mob action tailor-made for those few malcontents who desire a total breakdown of organized society (1967: 34346).

For Beatty, then, the dissent of the day transgressed a number of normative boundaries. Speech that ought to be rational and disembodied too easily spilled into action, action too easily disrupted the "intended use" of public space—intended, that is, for the use of a public constituted by Nixon's famous "Silent Majority"—and the content of speech itself too easily took on a deviant character when articulated by "bearded youth" uttering "four-letter words."

Like Byrd, Beatty's argument ultimately rested on a notion of citizenship fundamentally different from that articulated by the dissenters in the streets. Citizenship in this vision was not a bundle of rights always imperfectly granted by the state, but a set of duties and responsibilities to be performed [6]. As he put it, "[t]his country cannot accept a doctrine which allows a citizen to pick and choose the obligations of citizenship he will practice" (1967). To admit the notion that law—and by extension citizenship—was socially constructed was to invite anarchy. The understanding of public space was similarly bluntly commonsensical.

This line of argument—in which a duty-based understanding of citizenship and a "raceless" identity politics (Goldberg 2002) was used to interpret events in public space—was quite common in interpreting the significance of the riots. Indeed, Hoover argued a similar point when he said in an interview that "[w]e are living in an age when too many citizens are thinking about their rights and privileges and too little about their duties and responsibilities" (Beatty 1967). Here the duties and responsibilities to which Hoover was referring were those owed ultimately to the state as the bearer of the "public good."

Responsible citizens, critics charged, would not willingly engage in public protests, much less riots, without being coerced or otherwise incited to do so. The collective violence that erupted in city after city was thus not a legitimate expression of generalized black rage, but rather the influence of a conspiracy of individual malcontents who incited actions that otherwise would not have occurred. Along these lines, one South Carolina editorialist wrote that "the minority does not rise up spontaneously to parade, to demonstrate, and eventually to riot, without the aid of professional agitators" (O'Connor 1967). From this perspective, the moral lines that distinguished a parade from a demonstration or a riot were unclear at best, and the influences that moved the empirical phenomena from one to another not easily contained.

This editorial, entitled "The North Meets the Outsider," made clear the professional agitators in question were not only illegitimate by virtue of their "vocation" and politics, but also by virtue of their *geographic* origin. Authentic politics in this vision—which included authentic collective anger, presumably—was the province of the local. By placing agency elsewhere—in the bodies of deviant outsiders—critics sought to occlude any potential political meaning such events might elicit. The author's point in the editorial was that in the same way that Southern cities had previously been disrupted by the "outside agitators," Northern cities were now also the victims of these same individuals. If the North saw itself as above sectional finger-pointing, then it was only consistent to argue that the previous performances of dissent in the South were equally illegitimate. The editorial thus concluded that "[w]e sympathize with our northern brethren in their time of trial, but we find the methods by which they meet that trial unworthy of solid government and sound sense" (O'Connor 1967).

Law-and-order critics typically articulated the deviant outsider theme with reference to a national geography that opposed North and South, Big City from Small-Town America. Much of these arguments, of course, were wrapped up in the spatial politics of segregation that divided both the political space of the nation and the public spaces of Southern towns and cities. At times, however, the geography of identity politics was writ significantly larger. Far-right organizations like the John Birch Society depicted the unrest in U.S. cities as evidence of Communist conspiracy.

The film *Anarchy USA* (Griffen 1965) was one product of the conspiratorial Cold War geopolitical inflection of the outside agitator thesis. The film opens with images of a young man speaking before a crowd in Watts about moving out of the ghetto and going after white people, and then quickly cuts to an image of a black preacher in a church. The juxtaposition seems to suggest little difference between the two. The commentary then discusses unrest and riots elsewhere, explaining that "anarchy … was something we read about in our newspapers that was always happening in other countries. … It could never happen here."

The film then shows a series of news images of riots in the United States, culminating in a stream of images and commentary about Watts. The narrator explains the devastating impact of the violence in Watts and says that "the spectacle of American soldiers shooting it out with American civilians was even more shocking than the rioting itself." The film then presents viewers with an image of a newspaper headline that reads "Anarchy, USA," and the observation that "this time it wasn't a foreign country. This time it was Anarchy, USA." Noting the odd confluence of unrest in time and space, the narrator says that "it was as though an unseen hand had given the signal." The remainder of the film then presents an argument that a conspiracy of outside influence was responsible for the riots and that Civil Rights leaders like Martin Luther King were bearers of such subversive influence.

An only somewhat more subtle editorial from Decatur, GA, focused on Student Nonviolent Coordinating Committee leader Stokely Carmichael as an outsider not only by politics and geographic origin, but by origin of birth. Opening with the provocative statement that "[s]ome years ago a man wandered up from the country of Trinidad" (*Congressional Record* 1967a), the author writes that Carmichael "goes around the country preaching his doctrine of sedition, hate, insurrection, anarchy, murder, and arson." For this editorialist, Carmichael's deviance was not only because he was a black militant who seemed not to know his place, but because he was born elsewhere.

Reading the Riot Act: The *H. Rap Brown Act* and the Politics of Scale

> [T]he most serious domestic crisis facing America today is the ominous threat of riots and mob violence that hangs like a pall over many of our cities. We believe that the vast majority of the people share this opinion. ... The majority of the committee has responded to this crisis by ordering a bill which will give added protection to roving fomenters of violence, such as Stokely Carmichael and H. Rap Brown.
>
> — U.S. Senators James Eastland and Strom Thurmond (U.S. Senate 1967b: 15)

The enactment of this bill would cramp the style and make subject to criminal prosecution the Stokely Carmichaels, the Martin Luther Kings, the Floyd McKissicks, and others of their kind who preach anarchy and disobedience to the law.

— Congressman O. C. Fisher of Texas
(Remington 1973)

Perhaps the most fascinating geopolitical irony surrounding response to the riots was that of conservative Southern Congressmen who, while on one hand lambasting the illegitimate extension of federal authority over "states' rights" that surrounded civil rights measures, argued on the other for aggressive federal intervention to protect local communities against the threat of unrest. Representative William Cramer (D, FL)—one of the primary sponsors of the Federal *Antiriot Act* that emerged out Congressional debate on the issue of riots—argued for vigorous federal action to counteract the "outside agitators." As he put the matter, "more police officers and even improved riot control will be of little value when the Stokeley Carmichaels and H. Rap Browns and other professional rabble-rousers who are inciting these riots escape the jurisdiction of these local authorities and hide behind the protective shields of state borders" (1968).

Brown and Carmichael were the two men most frequently cited in Congressional debate as responsible for the riots that devastated city after city in the "long hot summers" of 1967 and 1968. Brown and Carmichael were charismatic, often polemical, leaders. Their politics reflected a turn in the Civil Rights movement away from the more accommodationist stand of Martin Luther King—and the nonviolent tactics that went along with it—towards a more militant black nationalism. Their focus was not on being granted the full rights of citizenship by a white majority, but rather to carve out a separate black public sphere in which black identity and citizenship were defined on their own terms. Brown argued, for example, that "[i]ntegration was never our concern" and that it was "impractical" (1969: 56). In his memoir *Die Nigger Die!* Brown illustrated his point with reference to the spatial politics of famous Civil Rights movement struggles. "I resented somebody telling me I couldn't eat at a certain place," he wrote, but "[i]t wasn't that I wanted to eat there" (1969: 56). Likewise, he argued that "[i]f I had a free choice I'd sit in the back of the bus" because "[t]hat's where the heater is." Their focus was not on the creation of an integrated society with integrated spaces—restaurants, movie theaters, busses, and public streets—but rather on what Brown explained as a desire to let "white folks know that they could no longer legislate where we went and what we could do" (1969: 56).

It was not just *what* Brown and Carmichael said that mattered, however, but *where*. When Brown, for example, said, "The streets are yours. Take 'em," he did so not on the static space of an editorial page, but rather on a platform in a ghetto in Cambridge, MD. Moreover, he did so just before the neighborhood erupted in a riot. Brown's speech—or rather a tape recording and transcript of it—made its way into testimony before the Senate Judiciary Committee as it was evaluating the appropriate federal response to riots such as that which took place in Cambridge. It was introduced by Cambridge Police Chief Bryce Kinnamon and played before the committee. The speech opened with Brown answering Langston Hughes' question, "What happens to a dream deferred?" with the claim that,

> Detroit answers that question. Detroit exploded. New York exploded. Harlem exploded. Dayton exploded. Cincinnati exploded. It's now time for Cambridge to explode, ladies and gentlemen (U.S. Senate 1967a: 31).

According to Kinnamon's testimony, upon finishing the speech, Brown led a group through the streets of Cambridge towards the business district, along the way "instructing them to burn and tear Cambridge down, to shoot any policeman who tried to interfere" (U.S. Senate 1967a: 31). As Kinnamon recounted, a riot began shortly thereafter. "I am confident," he concluded to the committee, "that his speech was the sole reason for our riot" (U.S. Senate 1967a: 38).

For conservative law-and-order senators, examples like this were proof enough that the dynamics of dissent had fundamentally changed for the worse and that strong federal intervention was needed in response. The result was the Federal *Antiriot Act*. Its sponsors sought to write the logics of the outside agitator thesis into law as a way to assert federal authority over the conduct of dissent in local public spaces. They did this by reworking the legal-spatial logics of the crime of incitement to riot, making what had historically been a local crime into one of national scope. The law targeted anyone "who travels in interstate or foreign commerce or uses any facility of interstate or foreign commerce, including, but not limited to, the mail, telegraph, radio, or television, with intent" to incite, organize, participate in, or in any way contribute to a riot (*Antiriot Act* 1968). The law, then, applied to explicitly public and collective expressions of either real or threatened violence. It applied to that realm of politics where the legitimate "protest" is marked off from the illegitimate "riot." And it worked its legal leverage precisely by blurring the distinction (itself blurred in reality) not just between the legitimate protest and the illegitimate riot, but between actual, bodily travel and the "facility of" such travel: the less tangible spaces of connection created by the television and radio signal and the telephone line.

How, then, did the authors of the *H. Rap Brown Act* envision the connection between individual intent and collective actions in space as they were played out in these riots? There were really two aspects to this question. The first involved assessment of what might be a called a micro-politics of bodies-in-space. This issue turned on one of language: What constitutes a riot? Historically, riots have typically been defined as three or more people "tumultuously" assembled in public space, involving violence against either people or property. Those responsible for the riot were in fact the actors who perpetrated the violence. The cause-effect relationship was a direct one and one localized in space.

The second issue involved a macro-perspective that linked thought and (bodily) action across space. Incitement to riot begins the abstraction process whereby speech can have indirect causal force. One can thus be prosecuted even if not directly involved in violent acts merely by establishing a relationship between public speech uttered by one actor (or group of actors) and actions enacted by another. This abstraction is at once spatial in nature, as intentional thought located in one place is projected with causal force to another.

Congressional debate around the definition of riot began with the traditional definition. The problem this presented for a federal antiriot law was how to establish a clear link between speech on one side of a political boundary and action on the other. Typically, incitement involved a quite localized spatial stage and almost immediate temporal cause-effect relationship. Someone stood up before a crowd and uttered inflammatory speech that could be directly linked to subsequent actions by others. To argue for an expansion of both the spatial and temporal scale of riot incitement was thus to fundamentally change the legal logics of the crime itself. Proponents of the bill thus sought to relax the narrowly drawn causal requirements.

Johnson's Attorney General Ramsey Clark argued that local laws were sufficient to the task of prosecuting instances of riot incitement and also cautioned that the blurred legal language of the proposed law raised constitutional questions. Without a clearly established connection between the intention to incite a riot and the overt actions to do so, the law could be used to blunt all manner of political speech and activity that had only very indirect relation to unrest and violence. Clark thus suggested an alternative definition that defined a riot in traditionally narrowly drawn terms but also limited it further by specifying it to cover groups of 20 or more bodies in space.

Despite Clark's warning, the bill's sponsors pushed it through Congress with the broader definition intact, attached as a rider to the famous *Civil Rights Act of 1968*. The political irony was striking, and Strom Thurmond—one of the most fervent supporters of a federal antiriot law—ultimately voted against it because it would mean voting for the extension of federal authority over, among other things, housing (Epstein 1970). Byrd supported it only grudgingly, feeling the housing provisions were too strong and the antiriot provisions too weak. The Federal *Antiriot Act* was signed into law in April of 1968, with its authors defining riot as

> a public disturbance involving (1) an act or acts of violence by one or more persons part of an assemblage of three or more persons, which act or acts shall constitute a clear and present danger of, or shall result in, damage or injury to property of any person or to the person of any other individual or (2) a threat or threats of the commission of an act or acts of violence by one or more persons having, individually or collectively, the ability of immediate execution of such threat or threats, where the performance of the threatened act or acts of violence would constitute a clear and present danger of, or would result in, damage or injury to the property of any other person or to the person of any other individual. (*Antiriot Act* 1968).

Like the traditional legal definition, a riot could consist of as few as three people. The antiriot law also included the typical "clear and present danger" qualifier so dominant in 20th century public forum law. The doctrine was designed to preclude government intervention into regulating speech. It was not enough to show the mere advocacy of violence, no matter how extreme. Rather, the legal test was whether speech led to actions that constituted a clear threat to the integrity of the state itself.

Also discussed during the hearings preceding passage of the act was the possibility it might be used to temporarily detain people during the course of a riot situation. One U.S. District Judge from Texas, for example, wrote to the Committee urging

> that the act be amended to require that anyone caught under or apprehended in the act of "inciting a riot," that the bail bond be in such an amount as to make sure that the accused be confined until such a time as the danger of riot has passed in whatever locality the riot may be imminent (in U.S. Senate 1967a: 8).

The act itself never included such language, but it was clearly envisioned by some as providing additional legal leverage to detain people during the course of unrest so as to help quell it.

The degree to which some perceived the act as a response to black militants was reflected in an alternative name attached to the legislation: the *H. Rap Brown Act* [7]. Supporters of the bill routinely named Brown and Carmichael—as well as moderate Civil Rights leaders like King—as the primary instigators of the riots, as well as the targets of the legislation. Then House Republican leader Gerald Ford was referring to these men when he said of the antiriot law, "If it does nothing but shut up the loudmouths, it will be helpful" (*Congressional Record* 1967b).

For many quite beyond black militants like Brown and Carmichael, the act was interpreted as a threat. Labor unions expressed concern that it would limit their organizing activities. The newsletter for the International Woodworkers of America, for example, published an editorial entitled *"Antiriot Bill Dangerous"* that expressed concern about the "built-in danger of this bill to the trade union movement." The editorial painted a hypothetical scenario in which a labor organizer crossed state lines to advise a local union on a strike that later turned violent. Under such a circumstance, the editorial argued, the organizer could be prosecuted under the antiriot law. Obviously responding to such concerns, the authors of the act made a point of noting that it excluded the "legitimate objectives of organized labor," with the caveat that they be "orderly and lawful." The authors of the act were also careful to ease the fears of those concerned that the act constituted a further undermining of states' rights already eroded through the Civil Rights years. The act made clear here that transgression of local and state law would remain the province of their respective legal authorities.

The Chicago Eight

In practice, the Justice Department first used the *H. Rap Brown Act* in *United States v. Dellinger et al.* to prosecute individuals involved in the events of Chicago, 1968. In the aftermath, critics chastised the Chicago police and Mayor Daley for their handling of the events. Yet many others supported them, blaming both the dissenters as well as the media for broadcasting protesters' perspective [8]. Chicago became something of a political Rorschach test for ideas about dissent and public space. Although the federal antiriot law was in force during the summer of 1968, Clark refused to prosecute anyone under the statute. The following year, the newly elected Nixon administration focused blame instead on the movement leaders. The violence on the streets of Chicago would not have occurred if the organizers had not willfully violated the law and challenged police to enforce it. Moreover, relying on the new law, they argued that the defendants' incitement of the riot was a product of their reliance on connections and resources that stretched far beyond Chicago itself. Their crime was thus federal.

Mobility, Public Space, and the *Antiriot Act*

Chicago's ultimate meaning was resolved in part in the high-profile legal trial *U.S. v. Dellinger*. The trial was partly a political show that the Justice Department used to dramatize its interest in shrinking the boundaries of dissent. It provided an object lesson for the public about the limits of legitimate dissent. It was also the first significant use of the federal antiriot law. By targeting high-profile New Left leaders—in this case the group that became known as the Chicago Eight—the government hoped to deter future unrest.

The trial was a spectacle from the beginning. The defendants were repeatedly reprimanded by the judge for their courtroom behavior. Abbie Hoffman blew kisses to the jury on the opening day of the trial and when asked while on the stand for his place of residence, he replied, "Woodstock Nation." Bobby Seale—the only black defendant—repeatedly asserted his right to represent himself in the trial and was ultimately ordered bound and gagged for his repeated outbursts, including calling the judge a racist. The defendants were ultimately convicted of violating the antiriot law and each sentenced to 5 years in prison and a $5,000 fine.

Much of the defense argument centered on the connection between citizenship, law, and space. Although the issue at stake was at its core about the limits of free speech in a democratic society, the defense team interpreted much of this issue with reference to the geographic conditions under which speech is uttered and invested with persuasive force. Speech does not exist in a vacuum, but rather establishes relationships among and between speaker(s) and audience. These relationships, lawyers argued, were fundamentally spatial relationships.

The legal brief submitted by the defense team for its appeal of the conviction included an extended analysis of the dynamics of scale and dissent, and of the manner in which the antiriot law attempted to intervene in these dynamics. "[A]t no time in the history of the nation," the defense team argued, "has legislation been enacted so bluntly and directly for the overt purpose of limiting freedom of speech and belief unhampered by concern for constitutional limitation" (Kinoy, Schwartz, and Peterson 1971: 41).

One focus of the appeal revolved around free speech and public space. What rights did the defendants have to assemble in Lincoln and Grant Parks if they had no legal permits to occupy these spaces? The issue was an important one because the plaintiffs argued that the activists' presence in the parks was illegal and that in forcibly removing people from those spaces, the police were merely enforcing the law. Here the defense drew on a 1965 ruling by the Supreme Court in *Shuttlesworth v. Birmingham*. That case had involved a Civil Rights march that took place without a permit. The court concluded that under conditions in which good faith efforts to obtain a permit were thwarted without reasonable explanation, citizens had a right to access those public spaces anyway. By drawing on this ruling, the defense sought to legitimize the activists' place in the parks and therefore to argue that any resulting violence was a product of the Chicago police's trampling of their constitutional rights of assembly.

As fascinating as this legal issue was, it was only indirectly related to the *Antiriot Act* per se, which was more substantially focused on the relationship between mobility and assembly. There, the defense argued the law was unconstitutional because of its overbroad definition of the crime in question: the riot. The brief painted the issue in sinister terms:

> The logical consequences of this astounding definition of "riot," a definition absolutely unique in either the common law or statutory history of the offense known as "riot," are frightening to contemplate. The harsh reality of contemporary American political life reveals that there is not a single manifestation of mass popular political expression which could not today fall within the broad prohibitory sweep of this extraordinary definition of "riot"(Kinoy, Schwartz, and Peterson 1971: 68).

Their concern was that the law failed to mandate explicit personal involvement in the violent unrest, or at least a direct relationship between intentional speech by an individual and violent action by others.

The defense then linked this definitional issue around the antiriot law to its spatial implications. The defense recognized that the broad definition of riot was necessary to the very logic of the bill in defining the crime as federal. The Chicago Eight were convicted of violating the *Antiriot Act* because of their intent to incite a riot upon crossing state lines. Yet intent under those circumstances could only be inferred based on their localized actions in Chicago. The Justice Department lawyers, for example, introduced testimony about public speeches made by the defendants in Chicago advocating violence as evidence of such intent. They never made any explicit connection between actions of the defendants and the subsequent actions of others. Moreover, such evidence alone failed to establish a federal jurisdiction.

Ultimately, the defense argued, by broadening the definition of riot the authors of the *Antiriot Act* sought to shrink the boundaries of legitimate dissent by shrinking the geographic realm in which activists could freely move. In particular, they focused on the essential spatiality of that fundamental precept of democratic society: freedom of expression. Free speech is inseparably linked to freedom of assembly, which in turn is closely linked to mobility rights. "The nexus between the right to travel and freedom of expression," the defense team argued, "lies in the very nature of expression itself." (Kinoy, Schwartz, and Peterson 1971: 99) Again, the defense relied on Supreme Court precedent to make this argument, in particular *Aptheker v. Secretary of State* and *Shapiro v. Thompson*. The first case involved a political radical whose passport was revoked by the State Department to preclude his travel outside the United States. The Court ruled that the State Department's actions in this circumstance constituted a violation of the defendant's constitutional rights: that they punished political ideology rather than criminal acts. The brief quoted Justice Douglas' concurring opinion:

> Free movement by the citizen is of course as dangerous to a tyrant as free expression of ideas or the right to assembly and it is therefore controlled in most countries in the interests of security. ... This freedom of movement is the very essence of our free society, setting us apart. Like the right of assembly and the right of association, it often makes all other rights meaningful—knowing, studying, arguing, exploring, conversing, observing, and even thinking. Once the right to travel is curtailed, all other rights suffer, just as when curfew or home detention is placed on a person (in Kinoy, Schwartz, and Peterson 1971: 99).

For the defense, mobility, speech, and citizenship were fused. They found support for this perspective in another Supreme Court ruling in *Shapiro v. Thompson*, where Justice Brennan wrote:

> This Court long ago recognized that the nature of our Federal Union and our constitutional concepts of personal liberty unite to require that all citizens be free to travel throughout the length and breadth of our land uninhibited by statutes, rules, or regulations which unreasonably burden or restrict this movement.

It is worth noting at this point that this case involved a rather different circumstance in which a woman was denied state benefits because she was a new resident, having previously moved from another state. I will return to the tensions between different legal framings of mobility in Chapter 6. Still, in this case, the defense argued that the Court's ruling reaffirmed that freedom of mobility was an implicit constitutional right.

The defense sought to show that the definition of riot written into law was overbroad to the degree that it could be easily used to punish thought rather than action, and that the effect was to limit constitutionally protected political activity by placing undue restrictions on the right to freely move. Moreover, movement under the antiriot law included not only the movement of bodies across space, but also the virtual movement of ideas and symbols across the airwaves. In an increasingly mediated world, such a law placed yet further restrictions on political activity. The public, put simply, is by definition somewhere else. As such, some kind of medium needed to facilitate the movement of ideas across space. "In a society where distances are large and access to the public media is essential to the effective communication of ideas," the brief continued, "freedom to move quickly from one part of the country to another is an essential ingredient of the effectiveness of First Amendment guarantees" (Kinoy, Schwartz, and Peterson 1971: 99–100).

The defense thus argued that essential political activity has *always* been bound up in worlds more expansive than the local. The geopolitical calculus behind the antiriot law, they argued, was an old one inseparably fused with "the concept of 'outside agitator'" (Kinoy, Schwartz, and Peterson 1971: 100). The very concept reflected an effort by those resistant to social change to close the gates around the local and to label as illegitimate such public dissent. Digging back in history, the brief explained that "so-called 'outside agitators'"

> have performed an indispensable function in our nation. From the Boston Tea Party to the streets of Selma, Alabama, their freedom to express their ideas, to seek change

and responsiveness on the part of government to the needs of the people, and to travel to every corner of the nation to do so, has long been the cornerstone of constitutional protections (Kinoy, Schwartz, and Peterson 1971: 103).

The nation itself, in other words, was founded by "outside agitators." "[F]reedom of expression," this argument concluded, "can know no boundaries, and people must be free to move across state lines and to use the facilities of interstate commerce for the purpose of speech, discussion, and 'agitation'" (Kinoy, Schwartz, and Peterson 1971: 106).

In this sense the Federal *Antiriot Act* attempted to keep people in their proper (and quite circumscribed) place by making use of existing political boundaries. "Unlike any other federal criminal statute which purports to meet and correct a social evil, the 'evil' here contemplated by those who drafted this legislation was 'freedom of movement' *itself*" (Kinoy, Schwartz, and Peterson 1971: 100). That such a politics of scale and publicity was understood in explicitly racial terms is clear enough from the testimony of its sponsors. The geographic problem the *Antiriot Act* was crafted to address was the public expressions of dissent by black Americans. Such dissent was waged over and in America's urban public spaces.

Ultimately, the defense argued that the antiriot law would limit constitutionally protected political activity. As they put it,

> as long as this statute stands no American can be confident that he or she can even participate in, no less organize, any mass demonstration involving controversial opposition to any policies of the government without fear of prosecution under the act (Kinoy, Schwartz, and Peterson 1971: 73).

The case of *U.S. v. Dellinger* seems to suggest just such an interpretation, as the instance in question involved an explicitly political event, and the defendants were high-profile political activists.

Containing Dissent

The *H. Rap Brown Act* was borne of a particular historical-geographical moment, one that put the nation-state itself—at least in the perception of many—at some peril. Such larger peril, in turn, was based on concern about a variety of people forcefully putting themselves in places they did not belong. The *H. Rap Brown Act* was thus a legal and spatial tool to control the public spaces of urban America. In more specific terms, the law, both in design and practice, was used to control dissent by New Left groups precisely by regulating the spatial field in which they moved. In crafting the bill, its authors proved themselves astute—if reactionary—interpreters of the spatial politics of the day: If a bunch of rabble-rousing communists and anarchists were striking at the very heart of the nation through their appropriations of public spaces, and if those actions depended on much wider nets of connection, the state should use federal authority—its command of national space—to cut those connections and thus circumscribe the realm of protest politics.

The hope of such a policy was that protest itself would wither away. Activist and Chicago Eight defendant David Dellinger later argued that the passage of the *Antiriot Act* was largely successful in limiting dissent. It "cut down," he argued, "the number of persons ready to commit themselves to antiwar organizing in the newer, more effective vein, particularly persons with regular jobs, family responsibilities, and more likely outreach to Middle America" (1975: 56). For Dellinger, the *Antiriot Act* effectively raised the stakes involved in confrontational protest politics, thus eliminating more mainstream activists from the performance of public dissent.

The antiriot law was not the only governmental product of 1968 and the concern about urban unrest. Like the *H. Rap Brown Act*, Operation Garden Plot had been drafted by military planners in 1968 to contain urban unrest. The plan specified general strategies such as the deployment of large numbers of troops, a focus on protecting life rather than property, and the establishment of curfews that allowed for the easy identification and control of deviant citizens, rabble-rousers, and so on. Garden Plot also included specific plans targeted to each prospective trouble spot (*U.S. News & World Report* 1968). These plans were drawn up based on detailed on-the-scene geographic research. Given the context out of which the plan emerged, it is no surprise that the focus was squarely on urban America. The first deployment of the plan, however, was not in the spaces for which it was intended—Los Angeles, Detroit, Newark—but in a decidedly marginal space, which we turn to in the next chapter.

4

Wounded Knee: Native Sovereignty and Media Spectacle

On 27 February 1973, approximately 200 American Indian Movement (AIM) activists and local residents began an occupation—ultimately to last 71 days—of the village of Wounded Knee, SD, within the boundaries of the Pine Ridge Indian Reservation. Within a short time, the Wounded Knee site was surrounded by an impressive show of government force: FBI agents and specially trained federal Marshals equipped with high-tech hardware provided, it was only later revealed, by the U.S. Army. Just as importantly, a virtual army of both domestic and international television and print reporters also surrounded the site.

As the site of a famous massacre of approximately 300 American Indian men, women, and children at the hands of U.S. soldiers in 1890, Wounded Knee was a particularly charged geographic symbol of the violence that accompanied American westward expansion and state building (Brown 1971). By claiming this famous historical site, the occupiers sought to raise awareness of American

Indian issues. More specifically and immediately, they sought to bring attention to, and ultimately remove, what they claimed was a corrupt reservation political structure. The occupiers were particularly concerned with the political rule of new Pine Ridge Tribal Chairman Richard (Dick) Wilson, whom they accused of corruption and of aggressively stifling political dissent. Such relatively modest goals, however, were tied into the far grander issue of treaty rights, the boundaries that spatially defined those rights, and the claims of sovereignty for which they stood. As such, the occupation questioned the very basis on which the most powerful nation-state in the world existed. The Wounded Knee occupation thus placed American state authority and national identity in radical question.

To make this point in clear language, on 10 March the Wounded Knee occupiers declared a new state: the Independent Oglala Nation (ION). Activists now declared the boundaries that defined this contested site "borders," whose status was to be aggressively maintained by a "border patrol." With dramatic images of Indian "warriors" occupying their bunkers to protect this territory (Figure 4.1) gracing the pages of major national magazines like *Newsweek* and *Time* (*Newsweek* 1973; *Time* 1973a, 1973b) and the screens of prime-time television, the Wounded Knee occupation was an early example of the power of mediated protest. Wounded Knee was what one commentator at the time referred to as "a test-tube case of confrontation politics and its symbiosis with the media" (Hickey 1973: 8) and what critics referred to as an example of "guerrilla theater." Writing in *The Nation*, for example, Desmond Smith (1973: 806) lamented that Wounded Knee constituted "an example of a new and expanding strategy of political manipulation that neatly circumvents the ordinary process of government [and] makes a direct and powerful appeal to the public through the mass media." Through AIM's successful "media coup"—in which reporters from all of the major news organizations in the United States, as well as a significant foreign contingent, quickly rushed to the scene of the story—Wounded Knee became "[o]vernight … the national headline and Washington found AIM's media gun pointed at its head" (Smith 1973: 808).

Fig. 4.1 Activists guarding perimeter of Wounded Knee occupation site. (Photograph courtesy of UPI/Corbis, used by permission.)

Because of this, the occupation also attracted the intense interest of the federal government, which responded with one of the most significant deployments of American state power in domestic space in the 20th century. For the White House, the Wounded Knee occupation was an issue of national concern. Although senior Washington officials tried to "low-key" the incident, as Attorney General Richard Kleindienst put it early in the occupation (Felt 1979: 268), they recognized their authority and responsibility to exert that authority in the "national interest." Particularly as media coverage and public attention raised the profile of the occupation, senior Washington officials insisted on a policy of restraint. In spatial terms, this policy was manifested in a strategy of containment. Rather than forcibly remove the occupiers, federal forces worked to limit the movement of people, things, and images back and forth across the boundary that defined the occupation site. Yet just as the conduct of the drawn-out occupation was fluid and changeable, so too was the status of the various boundaries that constituted the spatial form of this political spectacle. The contentious manner in which questions of authority and power on the Pine Ridge Reservation played out during the occupation was particularly apparent with respect to the various roadblocks and perimeters that determined who and what had access to Wounded Knee.

In this chapter, I analyze the complex geographical dynamics of this political event. By drawing, in particular, on the large collection of FBI documents made publicly available in the years since the occupation, I explain the actions and motivations of various state officials as they worked to manage a significant challenge to their authority. As a relatively early example of a televised protest—and because of the large number of documents available on the event—the Wounded Knee occupation sheds important light on the geographical dynamics of contemporary mass-mediated protest and on how states act in the context of such political spectacles. This chapter focuses in particular on how the issues of power and authority at the root of the conflict were played out over a series of boundaries that constituted this contested geographic space: what one government official referred to as a "protest platform." Such analysis, I argue, allows insight into not just this important historical event, but also broader issues of contemporary political protest and state power.

Mapping a Disorder, Containing Wounded Knee

The Wounded Knee occupation presented U.S. officials with a relatively new kind of political spectacle. Authority for government forces at Wounded Knee ultimately rested in Washington with the Attorney General formally, but only in close consultation with key Nixon White House staffers. In his memoirs, one of these staffers, Bradley Patterson, explained the general conditions that prompt White House involvement in domestic disorders. For the most part, he noted, the White House does not intervene in domestic crises, which are generally the province of local authorities. The White House may intervene in domestic crises "when they affect federal laws," however, and "*especially* when the perpetrators act under the banner of a cause which evokes widespread public sympathy—in America and overseas" (Hoffman 1973; quoted in Patterson 1988: 72). What distinguished these events for Patterson was their sheer spectacle: their scale-leaping, boundary-blurring use of mediated space. "The use of force may be threatened, and sometimes employed," he continued,

> but the confrontation is staged rather than waged, and it is mob leaders rather than marching armies who are raising hell. There is an element of guerrilla theater in such face-offs; the substantive cause or historical grievances may often be displaced or overwhelmed by the sheer drive for publicity for its own sake. The players then become actors on a world stage. Lenses, microphones, and newswires project the leaders' "demands" and all the on-scene developments to an intercontinental audience. ... Because of nationwide—in fact worldwide—attention ... such crises-as-theater ... escalate to White House control (ibid.).

Through new media technologies, activists changed the very nature of the political event. Protest now had the potential to become a theatrical drama. That dramatic quality, as well as the fact that the state was implicated in the drama, required active intervention to shape the public conduct of dissent.

Patterson's case study for just such acts was the Red Power Movement and what he called its "three-act drama": the takeovers of Alcatraz Island in 1969, the Bureau of Indian Affairs (BIA) headquarters in Washington in late 1972, and a few months later, Wounded Knee. All three takeovers took place under the Nixon administration, and the same administration officials handled all three at the White House level. All three "acts" also involved highly public spectacles of Indians occupying symbolic sites in order to make demands vis-à-vis the state. The Wounded Knee occupation was the final act of the drama. With Wounded Knee, what Patterson referred to as the "crisis-management machinery" of the state was above all managing a media spectacle in which the state's legitimacy itself was on center stage. Patterson noted that during the occupation a "Harris poll is published, disclosing that 93 percent of those questioned are following the Wounded Knee events and that 51 percent favor the Indian occupation." Patterson also noted the public looking on was not only national, but global. "Just how far-flung is the attentive public becomes clear," he suggested, "in a memorandum from the U.S. Information Agency"(Hoffman 1973; in Patterson 1988: 79), which stated that

> if Indians are killed, we can surely expect sharp and widespread foreign condemnation of this U.S. Government action. It would be a particularly unpropitious time, giving Arab governments an excuse to fog up the terrorist issue.

Wounded Knee represented—certainly for AIM, but also for the state itself—a challenge to federal authority. This challenge placed the legitimacy of the American state at issue on a global stage.

The occupation also raised similar issues for the state vis-à-vis a domestic public. In an article published in *Time* during the conflict, for example, one unnamed "administration official" claimed the occupation represented "an arguable case of treason" (1973a). "If we treat it like spitting on the sidewalk," he continued, "then the whole fabric of the country goes down the drain." For this official, the occupation of Wounded Knee was thus a political question only to the degree that it confused what for him was the more important conclusion: that it was a defiance of federal authority as codified unambiguously in law. Failure to deal firmly with such defiant illegality would only invite further such challenges in the future. As such, the state must use the occupation as an object lesson for the American public.

For White House officials like Patterson, however, the reality was far from unambiguous. Wounded Knee presented the state with an event that left open the question of where and how the line between political protest and illegitimate dissent was properly drawn. Because of the intense public attention in this occupation, and the broad public support *for* it—support that fundamentally understood Wounded Knee as a political event—Patterson's crisis-management machinery was dealing with both a law enforcement problem *and* a political problem.

Further, it was largely the media that served to publicly blur this distinction in practice. The state was thus also dealing with a public relations problem, which translated into a policy of restraint. The spatial expression of this policy of public restraint was a strategy of containment.

Defining a Protest "Platform"

The occupiers made claim to the Wounded Knee site through a range of tactics. AIM leaders knew their presence at Wounded Knee would continue only so long as they had the attention of "the public." Just as importantly, however, the occupation was constituted by a quite concrete reconfiguration of space. Teams of occupiers built bunkers and roadblocks of their own, both of which marked the boundary that delineated the space of the occupation. In a strategy at once symbolic and practical, road-blocks were constructed out of rusted and burned-out cars. The occupiers also used decoys, likely drawing on techniques of guerrilla warfare learned by veterans in Vietnam, to give the state a much-exaggerated impression of the weaponry available within Wounded Knee. At the same time, the occupiers and their sup-porters used various strategies to transcend those boundaries. The occupation could not be maintained without the ability to move people and things, ideas and images, back and forth across the boundary that defined the occupation site. One critic writing at the time in *The Nation* suggested that AIM's creation of a kind of semipermeable boundary influenced media coverage; as he put it, the occupiers "totally controlled the village of Wounded Knee, keeping the federal government out, but (by means of back trails) selectively allowing the press in"(Smith 1973: 808).

If AIM and its supporters worked to make Wounded Knee highly public and to extend its visibility as widely as possible, the state worked to contain the site and to minimize its visibility. Although ultimate authority for federal forces at Wounded Knee rested in Washington, in the hands of Attorney General Kleindi-enst, his Deputy Attorney General Joseph Sneed was responsible for day-to-day "policy formulation and decision making at the executive level" of the Justice Department during the occupation (SAC San Francisco 1973). The specific instruments available to Sneed included two separate divisions of the Department of Justice. The FBI's role during the occupation (and indeed, before) was to handle investigations of federal crimes. Within U.S. law, the federal government has jurisdiction on reservations for serious violations of law: murder, rape, and so on. The activists' burglary of the trading post and their seizure of hostages gave the FBI authority for criminal investigation. The U.S. Marshals took primary responsibility for establishing and maintaining the perimeter around Wounded Knee and the roadblocks that formed that perimeter.

Sneed himself, as he later explained to an FBI interviewer, "did not travel to Wounded Knee at any time [during the conflict], but conducted business pertaining to Wounded Knee at his Washington, D.C., office"(SAC San Francisco 1973). Although he had neither been to Wounded Knee, nor was involved in negotiating with the occupiers, Sneed explained to the interviewer that he retained two mementos of the experience: the first a document authored under his supervision called the *White Paper on Wounded Knee,* and the second "a map of the occupied area with lines of demarcation which he retained as a souvenir" (SAC San Francisco 1973). The map encapsulated in graphic terms the essence of the occupation. The *White Paper,* in turn, explained the map.

As the *White Paper* recounted, Sneed's initial spatial strategy was to contain the Wounded Knee site through the use of roadblocks and patrols as means to define an impervious perimeter. In the same way that the occupiers used a range of tactics to make use of various boundaries to further their ends, so too did federal representatives. They did this by limiting the flow of people, things, and symbols across the boundary established by the federal perimeter. If food and supplies could not make it into Wounded Knee, nor media images out, the standoff would end. Or such was the intent behind this strategy.

The result, however, was rather different than intended. Despite being surrounded by federal forces, the occupiers refused to accede to government demands. With the public attention on the occupation and the failure of negotiations, on 10 March federal officials decided to change spatial strategy and remove the roadblocks. According to the *White Paper*, there were two factors behind the strategy shift. First, the Justice Department recognized the materiality of the boundary, or more precisely, its *immateriality*. "The roadblocks," as they put it, "had not proven effective in halting the flow of men and supplies in and out of Wounded Knee." FBI Special Agent in Charge (SAC) Richard Held expressed concern that "because of the terrain it is entirely possible all of the Indians could slip out of Wounded Knee during the night and by tomorrow morning no one would be in Wounded Knee." Although he admitted this would pose no insurmountable problem in the long-term—that the FBI "could eventually locate the Indians"—such a "situation would be tremendously embarrassing" to the FBI and the U.S. government (Gebhardt 1973a). Likewise, federal attempts to exclude the media from Wounded Knee proved ineffective and led to the perception of censorship. With a large perimeter (20 km in circumference), officials recognized that it was impossible to completely seal access to Wounded Knee. The decision to remove the roadblocks was thus based on the quite-straightforward hope on the part of the Justice Department that "by lifting the roadblocks ... those inside Wounded Knee would come out and that the siege would be broken and that would be the end of that episode" (*United States v. Dennis Banks* 1974: 15,987).

A second, perhaps more important, factor was that the federal roadblocks had entered into the symbolic politics of the conflict. As explained in the *White Paper*, more than a question of dull practicality, the federal roadblocks "seemed to serve as a symbolic center for the occupiers' militance" (Department of Justice 1973a: xix). In later trial testimony, Sneed further explained,

> The whole occupation had a dramatic quality about it, and we felt that attempting to withdraw our roadblocks would—even if it failed—manifest a certain degree of flexibility on our part, which would not be lost upon the public (*United States v. Dennis Banks* 1974: 16,014).

The Justice Department was aware, through its keen attention to media coverage and opinion polls, not just that the conflict was being played out before a mediated public, but that it was *losing* this aspect of the conflict. Government actions were thus based on a calculation of how they would play on this very public stage.

In a particularly clear example of the more complex symbolic politics involved, Sneed was asked whether federal government actions with respect to its roadblocks were guided by the presumption that "certain options might permit the view or increase the view ... that the so-called occupation of Wounded Knee might be viewed or justified as an exercise of Indian self-determination on Indian land." (*United States v. Dennis Banks* 1974: 16,012). In response, Sneed explained,

> We were always aware of the dramatic quality of the occupation of Wounded Knee for Indians as well as Americans generally, and it's quite clear that it was necessary to demonstrate to the world as much restraint as we possibly could, while at the same time fulfilling the mission that had been assigned to us (*United States v. Dennis Banks* 1974: 16,013–16,014).

Early in the occupation the Justice Department became aware that the use of the federal perimeter to draw a line around the site of the occupation—both to mark that space as a site of disorder and rebellion and to quite literally contain it—helped to create the very spectacular space it was trying to close down. The Marshals and FBI agents who imposed and regulated this boundary were now wrapped up in a politics of publicity in which the state's own legitimacy was on stage.

Despite FBI concerns that the occupants would slip through the perimeter at nightfall, leaving federal forces an empty occupation site, AIM leaders were also interested in preserving the symbolic space created through these roadblocks and perimeters. An FBI report about an interview with one AIM representative in New York City noted his argument that the worst blow to Indian cause would be for all law enforcement officials to leave Wounded Knee and abandon efforts to subdue Indians there. Reasons are once pressure is off, government will do nothing to help Indians and Indians would look foolish occupying something no one cared about (Acting Director FBI 1973a: 3).

For all the symbolic spectacle of the event, both the activists who seized Wounded Knee and the federal officials trying to end the occupation recognized that a central aspect to the conflict was in the control of material space. "Wounded Knee," the Justice Department surmised, was now "a platform, a form of guerrilla theater" (Department of Justice 1973a: xxiv). This "platform" was certainly created and maintained by AIM and by the media, which projected its message everywhere. Yet, Sneed and other senior officials believed, they themselves also had a hand in creating the platform. The solution to this spatial problem was to dissolve the boundary that helped define the protest platform. With full confidence in the intelligence and law enforcement capabilities of the state, officials knew they could easily arrest people later. Before giving the order for the removal of the roadblocks, negotiators checked with one of the AIM security people to see if the move would elicit the desired effect. They were informed that the strategy would indeed work and that people would leave Wounded Knee once the roadblocks were removed.

A Declaration of Independence: Turning Perimeters into "Borders"

We no longer have a perimeter to defend—we have a border.

— Wounded Knee occupier (Anderson, Brown, Lerner, and Shafer 1974: 57)

For government officials, the end of the occupation seemed in sight as they removed federal roadblocks on 10 March.

Much to their consternation, however, the end was quite far off. Upon hearing news of the removal of the federal roadblocks, AIM leader Russell Means later recalled,

> Everyone was ecstatic … [but] I was very worried, and I almost panicked. When I could be heard, I said, "Look, it isn't over. Don't leave, because if you do they'll arrest you." Many of the Oglala people said they felt they needed to go home and check on their wives and husbands and children. I kept saying, "Wait! They're going to arrest you all!"(Means and Wolf 1995: 270–71).

Means' plea was initially ineffective, and many left with the removal of the federal roadblocks. Yet Means and many others stayed. As he continued,

> People were streaming out of Wounded Knee, but the next day even more began to pour in. They were men and women who had driven night and day from every corner of America, mostly from other Indian nations, but also a few whites, Asians, and blacks. Altogether, about 200 Oglalas went home, but in their place came about 150 other Indians. Most of the whites and some Indians were from Vietnam Veterans Against the War, including guys in wheelchairs who had been crippled or had lost limbs (Means and Wolf 1995: 271).

Not only had Means and other occupiers refused to leave with the removal of the federal roadblocks, but they and their supporters brought in more people and supplies in order to buttress the occupation materially and bodily.

It was in *this* context that the occupiers declared an independent state. As Means' explained, "We still hadn't forced the government to enter into real negotiations about treaty rights"(Means and Wolf 1995: 271). To do just that, in response to the removal of the federal roadblocks, the occupiers issued their declaration of the Independent Oglala Nation. The perimeter around Wounded

Knee was now declared a "border," whose integrity was maintained by a "border patrol."

This point was made clear on 11 March, when four postal inspectors, upon hearing news reports of the end of the siege, approached the village to ascertain the steps needed to re-establish mail service (Dewing 1995). There four Indians guarding their new "border" met them and took them into custody, believing them to be "spies." The postal inspectors were shortly thereafter joined by two ranchers who decided to pass through the village upon rumors that the occupation had ended. Means took advantage of this opportunity to make clear the status of the boundary around Wounded Knee. "Without a confrontation to focus public attention on Wounded Knee," he later recalled, "the government could ignore us." The new hostages/prisoners allowed just this sort of spectacle. Displaying them before news cameras, Means announced his intention to deal harshly with any other "foreign" intruders who crossed the "border" that defined the ION's sovereign space (Smith and Warrior 1996: 218).

With the arrests of the six hostages and the obvious failure of the occupiers to leave, Sneed ordered the federal roadblocks reinstated on 12 March. The standoff dragged on for another two months, with a contest over boundaries continuing to be central. The federal roadblocks themselves, in particular, remained a subject of government strategy, as well as political contention. Chief Marshal Wayne Colburn told reporters that "[w]e're planning to change their lifestyle" (Smith and Warrior 1996: 219). Federal forces tightened their perimeter and cut phone lines, electricity, and water service to Wounded Knee.

As federal forces tightened their perimeter, they also subjected media personnel to increasingly tight regulation. "AIM lives on good press coverage," as BIA Superintendent Stanley Lyman observed at the time, "even as it lives on food" (1991: 129). On 21 March, the government instituted a policy that barred media access to Wounded Knee after 4:30 p.m. each day. Whether intentional or not is unclear, but the exclusion of media from Wounded Knee at night "prevented them from observing the nightly meetings and firefights"(Anderson, Brown, Lerner, and Shafer 1974: 122). At the same time, government media handlers dramatically limited *which* media personnel were allowed any access at all. Press access was regulated through government-granted press passes. Now passes were only issued to media personnel from major networks. The alternative press was increasingly barred from the area. Ultimately, the major networks themselves were barred.

In the two weeks after the declaration of the ION, federal forces increasingly limited the flow of food and medical supplies to Wounded Knee, and the occupiers grew increasingly hungry. Likewise, with the exclusion of the media from Wounded Knee, the flow of images out of the site was also dramatically reduced. AIM leader Dennis Banks explained the effect in a meeting within Wounded Knee:

> They're stopping all the news media. They let in our lawyers when *they* want to. They let in a little bag of groceries when *they* want to. If we fail to correct that kind of policy somebody is going to get shot. They're steadily trapping us into a situation that's going to be very dangerous (Anderson, Brown, Lerner, and Shafer 1974: 116).

The state's intensified containment of Wounded Knee was designed to force a negotiated end to the occupation. For the occupiers and their supporters, as well as media personnel, access into and out of Wounded Knee was now limited to that which they could manage covertly.

A "Legal Assault" and a "Citizens' Roadblock"

To address the state's increasingly tight control of the occupation site, on 22 March a group of lawyers announced the formation of the Wounded Knee Legal Defense/Offense Committee. Responding to what they referred to as "a legal reign of terror operating in the midst of a para-military encirclement of the Wounded Knee community," the Committee promised "a massive legal assault against the federal government [and] its hired guns operating with armed personnel carriers [APCs] and helicopters." This effort would continue, they announced, "until South Dakota begins to look more like America and less like war-torn South East Asia" (Wounded Knee Legal Defense/Offense Committee 1973). To this end, the Committee's first action was to file suit against the government, with the intent to dissolve the boundary established by the state around the Wounded Knee site. Without food and supplies, the occupation could not continue. The Committee's legal strategy was thus to request judicial assistance to force federal forces to loosen their blockade. In response, on 25 March South Dakota Federal District Judge Andrew Bogue issued a temporary order that directed that six carloads of food and supplies, along with lawyers, be allowed through the roadblocks into Wounded Knee each day for the remainder of March (Anderson, Brown, Lerner, and Shafer 1974: 124).

At this point the Justice Department's frustration was evident, particularly so with the FBI. Mark Felt explained bluntly in a memo to FBI Acting Director Patrick Gray that the court order meant that "the situation at Wounded Knee has deteriorated beyond our control" and suggested that "we cannot continue to justify our present strike force and propose to withdraw all agents from roadblocks" (Felt 1973a). Felt had been opposed to the White House-directed strategy of containment from the beginning of the occupation (1979). Particularly bothersome to Felt, and to other FBI officials, was that FBI personnel were ordered to guard the roadblocks, which he believed beneath the agency. Equally significantly, however, FBI officials argued for more aggressive action to end the occupation, something that Judge Bogue's extension of federal judicial authority over the conflict appeared to cast in doubt.

As much as Felt and other senior government officials were bothered by Judge Bogue's court order, the tribal government was perhaps even more frustrated. Although the Wounded Knee conflict tended to be represented as one that pitted the Indians against the U.S. state, it was also significantly a battle *among* Indians. Although this battle was about identity and the politics of Indianness, it was equally about issues of power and authority, and the reservation as the space over which that battle was waged. Who had what authority over this space?

Like Washington officials, Pine Ridge Tribal Chairman Wilson recognized the seizure of Wounded Knee as a challenge to his authority. Unlike those officials, however, he was little concerned with exercising restraint before wider publics. Drawing on a conspiratorial Cold War geopolitical discourse, Wilson and his supporters represented the occupation as part of a sinister global conspiracy that placed the reservation under threat from outside. For the most part, they focused their attention on AIM as constituting this invading force. Although also drawing on an American nationalist discourse, Wilson and supporters defined the issues dramatized on the Pine Ridge Reservation in ways that served to justify their control of this local space. Wilson and supporters represented the reservation as the authentic preserve of those who supported the tribal government. Those aligned with AIM, by contrast, were represented as "outsiders." "[W]e don't have too many AIM people around here," the secretary to the tribal court explained during the occupation. "Most of the ones in Pine Ridge are outsiders," she continued, "and we *hate* people coming in from the outside telling us what to do" (*Time* 1973c).

For Wilson and supporters, federal negotiators were far too accommodating to the occupiers. More importantly from Wilson's perspective, perhaps, the decision-making of senior Washington officials did not include him. These conflicts came to a head around the subject of the federal roadblocks. Already frustrated with what he saw as the excessive restraint of federal forces at Wounded Knee, Wilson was infuriated by the ruling by an off-reservation federal judge to allow food and supplies into the occupation site. In response, the tribal government and the right-wing vigilantes aligned with it established roadblocks of their own in direct, and quite deliberate, violation of the court order. The logic on which this "tribal roadblock" was established was clearly articulated in two documents. The first, a 16 March tribal court order, put into legal terms the geopolitical discourse of Wilson's regime. Declaring a "state of emergency," the court ordered the expulsion of all outsiders who, as the order put it, "are hindering the interests of the Pine Ridge Reservation" (Oglala Sioux Tribal Council 1973). In turn, they demanded federal assistance in enforcing the order. On 19 March Wilson and the tribal government sent a letter to senior Washington officials in both the Department of Interior and the Justice Department (Wilson, Eagle Bull, and Nelson 1973). "We can no longer condone the attitude of the Department of Justice," the letter explained,

> or the fact that they do not wish to tarnish their image in the eyes of the American public by using necessary force in bringing the Wounded Knee situation to an end. ... We now request, insist, and demand, that the Department of Justice revert to its basic role as a law enforcement agency and do whatever is necessary to implement the provisions of [the Tribal Ordinance] ... and bring an end to this civil disorder and state of emergency caused by the occupation of the Wounded Knee site by this militant and seditious group.

The letter asserted tribal government authority over Pine Ridge and argued that the Justice Department should be placed at its service.

Even if the Justice Department agreed to assist Wilson, it had little control over a federal judge. In response to the 25 March Federal District Court order a few days later that allowed precisely the outsiders the tribal government worked to keep out not only to cross reservation boundaries but to enter the Wounded Knee site itself, Wilson and supporters acted quickly to enforce their control of reservation boundaries. The logic was explained in a newsletter distributed to supporters. Addressed to "fellow Oglalas and fellow patriots," the newsletter explained in the following way the context as it stood in late March and how the "good citizens of the Pine Ridge Reservation" planned to respond:

> The time has come for all good citizens of the Pine Ridge Reservation to lay aside their petty differences and squabbles and unite. Unite against the American Indian Movement

and their planned takeover of our reservation. What has happened at Wounded Knee is all part of a long-range plan of the Communist Party. ...To combat this unpleasant nuisance we are confronted with, Oglalas, we are organizing an all-out volunteer Army of Oglala Sioux Patriots. We need all able-bodied men over the age of 18 years. The supporters of AIM come in all shades and the National Council of Churches are very vocal because the Liberal Press and the T.V. News media is right at their elbow. ...Since the American Indian Movement at Wounded Knee is supported by non-Indians, we are enlisting the help of all non-Indian residents of the Pine Ridge Reservation (Wounded Knee Legal Defense/Offense Committee Records 1973).

At once nationalist and localist in orientation, the newsletter made clear who properly belonged on the reservation and who did not. Anyone who supported or was sympathetic to the occupation was marked as an outsider. Wilson rejected even the federal judicial authority represented by the court order with an assertion of tribal sovereignty. When AIM lawyers approached Wilson's roadblock with the injunction, he told them, "That does not apply here in Indian country" (*Newsweek* 1973).

With the "tribal roadblock"—also called the "citizens' roadblock" by reservation supporters—such geopolitical discourse was given spatial form. Beginning on 26 March gun-toting volunteers and members of a private security force called the Guardians of the Oglala Nation—referred to as the GOON squad—assembled, beyond the federal roadblocks, on the key road leading to Wounded Knee. Their immediate strategy was to control who had access into and out of Wounded Knee and to ensure the food and supplies allowed into the site by Judge Bogue never arrived.

Wilson's establishment of the tribal roadblock put him into direct conflict with both the Justice Department and the federal judicial system. This placed federal forces on the scene who enforced federal authority in an awkward position. Despite defying federal authority, officials initially allowed the tribal roadblock to stand. Although those operating the roadblock were threatened with arrest on a few occasions, "[n]o federal forces were used against them" (Dewing 1995: 98). As the conflict dragged on over the next month, and Wilson supporters continued to erect their roadblock and otherwise interfere with federal forces at Wounded Knee, the issue of who had what authority on the reservation was again raised with respect to the tribal roadblock. On 23 April members of the tribal roadblock detained federal representatives of the Justice Department's Community Relations Service (CRS). BIA Superintendent Lyman explained the conflict over CRS personnel:

> These are people who, as [tribal secretary] Toby Eagle Bull informed us, are not federal employees but are here under contract to the government. Their purpose is ostensibly to communicate with the people of both sides, but they have endeared themselves to AIM and are disliked by the local people displaced from Wounded Knee. The government wants them treated like part of the Justice Department and insists that they be allowed to enter the occupied area. The tribe and the men on the roadblock do not regard them as such and refused to allow them to pass (1991: 109).

The official in charge of U.S. Marshal personnel at Wounded Knee, Chief Marshal Colburn, had little patience for such selective respect for federal authority. On instructions from Sneed to dismantle the tribal roadblock, Colburn angrily confronted roadblock members and subsequently arrested 11 of them. As an FBI report on the event explained, "There is no longer an Indian roadblock" (Anderson, Brown, Lerner, and Shafer 1974: 189).

Colburn's dissolution of Wilson's instrument to reassert his authority over the reservation was rather short-lived, however. That same night, in fact, Wilson's men again erected the roadblock. Once again the Marshals dismantled it. The next morning, on 24 April, Wilson, accompanied by a large group of supporters, went to the tribal roadblock area to confront the Marshals. Colburn was unwilling to back down and threatened to use tear gas to disperse the crowd if necessary. Amid this tense circumstance, according to one FBI report on the incident, "SAC Held [then] arrived on the scene and calmed a heretofore volatile situation" (Federal Bureau of Investigation 1973).

Another FBI document, a memo from Felt, discussed more fully the conflicts over the tribal roadblock (1973b). The confrontation, Felt argued, was "a tempest in a teapot": a "head-butting contest between the Oglala Sioux on one side, and the Marshals Service and the Community Relations people on the other side." In describing the confrontation this way, Felt was attempting to place the FBI as the dispassionate observer, dedicated to preserving law and order and unconcerned with such trivialities. What is evident in Felt's description of the conflict between Indians operating the tribal roadblock and U.S. Marshals attempting to remove them, however, is the contention among different organizations *within* the state, even within the Department of Justice. Claiming insufficient personnel and that "they had no responsibility for containment or protection"—a duty specified to the Marshals—Felt instructed agents on the scene "not to take any action involving physical force to prevent these Indians from moving back into position" at the roadblock. When the Deputy Attorney General subsequently instructed the FBI to take over such responsibility for "containment and protection in the area of [the federal] roadblock ... [and] take every possible action to insure that the Oglala Sioux roadblock is not re-reestablished," Felt (obviously splitting hairs) then explained to the SAC at Wounded Knee that this "would not include responsibility for physically preventing the re-establishment of the [tribal] roadblock several miles away" (1973b).

Felt's reluctance to fully implement the orders from above reveals a more complex story about the FBI's position with respect to the politics of the occupation. In further discussing the instructions of Deputy Attorney General Sneed with the SAC at Wounded Knee, the latter explained that he would be willing "to move in and replace the Marshals and control the situation," provided that both Chief Marshal Colburn and members of the Community Relations

Service be removed from Wounded Knee. The request was then relayed to Acting Director Gray, who suggested it to Sneed. Sneed, however, refused to approve the request. He did, however, agree to remove Colburn from the scene of the immediate controversy over the roadblock.

It was in *this* context that "SAC Held arrived on the scene"—in rather dramatic fashion, no less, by helicopter—"and calmed ... [the] volatile situation" (Anderson, Brown, Lerner, and Shafer 1974: 193). The FBI's actions with respect to the tribal roadblock were thus hardly as dispassionate and politically neutral as their reports suggested. BIA Superintendent Lyman explained exactly how the FBI stepped into the situation:

> The end result was that the FBI, who had been directed to maintain responsibility on [the federal] roadblock, ... quietly extended their jurisdiction down the road just a little bit to include the site of the citizens' roadblock. There the FBI set up their own roadblock and invited the Indians into it (1991: 112).

In essence, the FBI's political position was to side with the tribal government. On the other hand, and inseparably, the FBI was in a head-butting contest of its own with other divisions within the Department of Justice: both the Community Relations Service and, more significantly, the U.S. Marshals [9]. This point was clearly illustrated in the directions of FBI Acting Director Gray that, as Felt explained, the SAC at Wounded Knee was "to take over from the Marshals and take every possible step to control the situation, and at the same time avoid confrontation" (Felt 1973b).

The conflict over the roadblocks—and the confusion—continued the next day (25 April), however. At a press conference, a reporter asked Deputy Assistant Attorney General Richard Hellstern—the Justice Department's then-senior official at Wounded Knee—why Indians continued to operate roadblocks that were determining who had access to Wounded Knee. Unaware of the FBI's actions, Hellstern replied "there are no Indians on that roadblock"

(Lyman 1991: 113), to which reporters explained they had seen them with their own eyes. As Lyman recounted, "Hellstern was so concerned about this that he left the press conference and went upstairs" to confirm the information. Hellstern had given the orders to Chief Marshal Colburn to dismantle the tribal roadblocks, even if it required tear gas (Anderson, Brown, Lerner, and Shafer 1974: 193). After returning to the press conference with the information that the roadblock in question was "an FBI roadblock; it is ours" (Lyman 1991: 113), Hellstern, along with senior Justice Department official Kent Frizzell and Colburn, went to the roadblock to see the situation firsthand. Lyman explained what they found upon arriving:

> When they arrived at the roadblock they were met by a 17- or 18-year-old Indian boy armed with a double-barreled shotgun. He rapped on the window of the car and said, "Roll down the window." Here were individuals of authority and responsibility, men accustomed to giving orders and making challenges; now they were being inspected and challenged themselves. The Marshal bounded out of the car with what some said was an M-1 carbine, others an M-16. The Marshal with his rifle and the Indian kid with his shotgun faced each other at gunpoint (1991: 114).

As Wilson later put it at a news conference, "We came this far from shooting Frizzell and Colburn" (Smith and Warrior 1996: 255).

State Power, Privacy, and Scale at Wounded Knee

If the Wounded Knee occupation had solely played out before network television cameras and simply revolved around the question of who had what visible control of the space around the occupation site, events might have turned out differently than they did. Instead, the Justice Department, in conjunction with the U.S. Army, used two tactics that significantly contributed to their ability to contain the event, but went little noticed in the press. The public invisibility of these deployments of state power was, in fact, precisely by design and accounted in large part to their success. It also helps further illuminate the dynamics of the occupation and with it the larger concerns of this book.

The H. Rap Brown Act at Wounded Knee

A fact little reported at the time in the media, nor commented on significantly in the academic literature since, was the state's wide-scale use of the *H. Rap Brown Act* as a tool to contain the Wounded Knee conflict. "With hundreds of people facing substantial prison terms," one group argued at the time, "the government is now preparing the second massacre of Wounded Knee, the one it hopes will take place in the courts. The weapons this time are the conspiracy and federal anti-riot laws" (Wounded Knee Information and Defense Fund 1973). "The Thurmond rider," another noted, "is coming into increasing use as a weapon to crush dissent," with "the takeover-protest at Wounded Knee" resulting in "the most massive use of the Federal *Antiriot Act* yet seen" (National Committee Against Repressive Legislation 1973).

Although the FBI had been investigating AIM members for antiriot violations prior to Wounded Knee, their efforts were stepped up with the occupation. Evidence suggests that the FBI began with a fairly limited target of investigation. Early instructions tended to focus on the transport of firearms across state lines. Yet other instructions, particularly beyond the first couple of weeks of the occupation, reveal a broader strategy of targeting any and all support. The timing appears not to have been a coincidence. The mediated spectacle of Indians occupying Wounded Knee against the might of the U.S. state had brought national and international attention as well as tangible support. Protests were taking place throughout the country in support of the occupiers, and people—schoolchildren even—were sending food and supplies to Wounded Knee to express their support.

The FBI tended to represent this support in quite sinister terms. On 16 March, FBI Acting Director Gray sent a letter to Attorney General Kleindienst, the substance of which he also relayed to Nixon Domestic Affairs Advisor John Ehrlichman.

This letter explained the national context of support as it related to Wounded Knee and began with an observation about "the increasing buildup of support around the country for the Indians." Gray continued by explaining the geography of this support:

> This support, in addition to generally peaceful demonstrations, which have been held in approximately 18 cities, is primarily manifested by an increasing number of reports of travel by dissident Indians and others to Wounded Knee for the purpose of aiding the Indians there. If this buildup of support at Wounded Knee continues, and reports indicate it is increasing, it could represent a serious danger to the security of Federal authorities and law enforcement personnel on the scene (Acting Director FBI 1973b).

Particularly striking was the connection Gray drew between mobility and threat. The Wounded Knee occupation was not a strictly local concern, and for the FBI to effectively deal with this fact, its field of vision needed to extend far beyond the occupation site itself.

Illustrating continuities with its efforts to subvert the Civil Rights and antiwar movements in the previous decade (Churchill and Vander Wall 1988; O'Reilly 1989), the FBI seemed particularly attentive to any kind of coalition across racial boundaries. "Black extremists and revolutionary white groups and individuals," one teletype explained, "have recently taken active parts in demonstrations around the country in support of the American Indian takeover at Wounded Knee." Given this context, Gray issued instructions "to alert all offices to this growing involvement" and to collect information regarding "all instances of support, financial or otherwise" (Acting Director FBI 1973c). In particular, Gray suggested agents look to use the legal-geographic tool of the *Antiriot Act* to preclude such a politics of connection.

According to American Indian scholar and AIM activist Ward Churchill, the FBI's expanded use of the *H. Rap Brown Act* came around 20 March (Churchill and Vander Wall 1988: 424n77).

A 22 March letter from Sneed explained quite clearly the logic on which the expanded use of the act rested. The Department, Sneed explained, was "desirous to prevent subversive elements from supporting the militant Indians" at Wounded Knee and instructed the FBI "that arrests be made at distant points where there is probable cause Federal law has been violated" (Assistant Attorney General 1973a: 2). In the words of the FBI's Acting Director, "The object" was "to make lawful arrests as far from Wounded Knee, South Dakota, as possible" (Acting Director FBI 1973d: 2).

And the FBI did just that. During the period of the occupation, more than 50 arrests were made in states throughout the country (Fishlow 1973). The strategy was quite simple: Where probable cause was established that a group of individuals appeared intent on offering support to the Wounded Knee occupants, agents were to monitor and carefully track their movements and arrest them, as one FBI report put it, "once [the] vehicle crosses the state line" (Portland 1973). Bail was also often set high to immobilize potential supporters. When they could not establish probable cause, Gray instructed his agents that "these groups are to be put under physical surveillance 24 hours a day" (Acting Director FBI 1973d: 1–2). "[I]n no way was there any indication of activities illegal in themselves," one critical press report noted at the time, "and in every case the only 'overt act' was getting on a federal highway and crossing a state line. As it was, they never did anything but travel" (Fishlow 1973: 12).

While continuing to investigate and arrest people throughout the country for violations of the *H. Rap Brown Act* through the rest of March and into April, however, the FBI encountered problems. First, the strategy was not entirely successful. Despite use of the act and other measures designed to limit movement into Wounded Knee, it remained impossible to completely seal access to the site. One FBI report noted that members of Vietnam Veterans Against the War (VVAW) had been successful in bringing supplies to Wounded Knee, a feat accomplished by minimizing *visible* travel. The report, itself the product of undercover investigation, revealed that "supplies would be transported [to Wounded Knee] by separate passenger vehicles rather than using a van or truck which law enforcement agencies could surveil" (St. Louis 1973: 1).

A second problem was a legal one. The 25 March federal court order to allow food and supplies to the occupiers had challenged at least the spirit of the strategy. But the FBI appears to have been unperturbed. A teletype from Gray, dated 27 March and distributed to FBI offices nationally, made mention of the court order, yet explicitly stated that "the court order is not being interpreted as preventing enforcement of [the antiriot law] in instances where individuals undertake interstate travel to render personal or material support to the occupiers of Wounded Knee" (Acting Director FBI 1973e). The expanded use of the antiriot law appears to have violated at least the spirit of the court order, because both the roadblocks and the *Antiriot Act* were designed to achieve the same purpose: to limit support for the occupation. Nevertheless, the FBI continued to investigate and arrest people.

If there was a latent legal tension evident between the federal court order and the FBI's use of the *H. Rap Brown Act*, by mid-April this tension was made overt. On 16 April, five people arrested for *Antiriot Act* violations filed suit against the FBI in a federal district court in Portland, OR, claiming "false arrest and conspiracy to deprive us of our constitutional rights" (Richmond 1973). The American Civil Liberties Union (ACLU) sponsored the suit, using it as a vehicle to challenge the constitutionality of arresting and prosecuting individuals under the *Antiriot Act* and "to deter others [agents] from such acts" (Remington 1973). At issue, the ACLU explained, was a Supreme Court interpretation of "a constitutional right to travel 'uninhibited by statutes, rules, or regulations which unreasonably burden or restrict this movement.'" The ACLU then linked this argument about the "right to travel" to that of the freedom of speech. If the architects of the *Antiriot Act* sought to keep people in their place by erasing the distinction between thought and deed, body and symbol, the virtual and the material, while collapsing the social into the individual—and in so doing, turned the resulting legal geography to a decidedly reactionary end—the ACLU intended to keep these distinctions alive.

The grand legal confrontation never happened, however, and both suits were ultimately dropped. Yet for some senior FBI officials, the lawsuit raised concerns about the legality of their actions. Referencing the Portland suit, Felt explained to Gray that

> the FBI ... is perhaps in an untenable position in arresting individuals far removed geographically from Wounded Knee based on the information that those individuals are en route to Wounded Knee for delivery of material to the dissidents there who are defying federal authority. Because of the very nature of this situation we necessarily are operating on probable cause that is extremely vulnerable to challenge (1973c).

Felt raised broader concerns about the manner in which the FBI deployed the *Antiriot Act*. The FBI, after all, was responsible for investigating and arresting violations of the act. Further, it was just these FBI personnel who were now being sued by citizens arrested with this strategy. Continuing, Felt urged,

> We should closely re-examine our position with regard to the arrests of individuals based on information that they are en route to Wounded Knee, particularly as in the Portland case where the individuals are hundreds of miles from their alleged destination.

FBI Acting Director Gray also expressed frustration and concern over the "extensive expenditure of manpower and that some of the cases ... are being dismissed," and asked Deputy Attorney General Sneed "to advise if it desires this Bureau to continue to vigorously investigate each and every possible violation of the antiriot law statute in connection with the Wounded Knee situation" (Acting Director FBI 1973f).

In reference to Felt's concerns regarding the Portland suit, the Assistant Attorney General explained to Gray on 16 April "that to avoid further exposure to civil actions, we will, if circumstances permit, attempt to secure arrest warrants ... prior to making any apprehensions" (Assistant Attorney General 1973b). Responding to concerns about personnel and less-than-vigorous prosecution, Sneed instructed Gray to "continue to vigorously investigate each and every possible violation of the antiriot law statute in connection with the situation at Wounded Knee" (1973). It "is the Department's intention," he explained, "to vigorously prosecute" such violations.

A third, but closely connected, problem presented itself the next day. In the early morning hours of 17 April, three small aircraft, operating from a "small remote airfield," successfully evaded the FBI's national security net and air-dropped food and supplies on Wounded Knee (Zimmerman 1976). The perimeter established by the state around the site, of course, offered little resistance to such aircraft, and because it entered the Wounded Knee area at daybreak, federal forces were caught by surprise.

This event highlighted, as the Justice Department put it, the "unique investigative problem" of the "numerous small aircraft … which can operate from small remote airfields" (Department of Justice 1973b). In order to address their concern about small aircraft that could slip under the eyes of the state, the Justice Department opted for a change in strategy with respect to its use of the *H. Rap Brown Act*. In response to the airdrop, and in the wake of the filing of the Portland lawsuit, the Department of Justice prepared to go public with its strategy, which until then had been effective largely because it had been kept relatively private. On 19 April, the Department issued a news release with the following warning:

> Persons who carry food, medical supplies, ammunition, or any other supplies to South Dakota by land or air for the use of the riotous occupiers of Wounded Knee are subject to federal prosecution (Department of Justice 1973b).

The reasoning behind the release was not, interestingly enough, to warn potentially ignorant citizens of unwittingly violating federal law. Rather, the intent was to enlist the support of what the release referred to as "the average law-abiding citizen" in "furnishing information concerning persons and groups moving in aid of the militants at Wounded Knee." As it had done so often in the past (Churchill and Vander Wall 1988; O'Reilly 1989), the state cleanly distinguished the deviant citizen, and sought to use "the public"—constituted by legitimate, "law-abiding" citizens—as a supplement to the imperfect resolution of its intelligence gaze. All of this was designed to limit the movement, and hence power, of the "militants" and "revolutionaries" moving across the nation with reckless abandon. By "going public," the Justice Department hoped a more informed public could help to better implement its strategy of arresting people at "points far removed geographically from Wounded Knee."

State Violence and Publicity: Operation Garden Plot

Another consequence of the 17 April airdrop was that it sparked a firefight. One woman explained:

> Ten bundles were pushed from the planes and floated down on colorful parachutes. ... [I]t turned out to be food airlifted to us by people in the antiwar movement who enclosed a letter of support and praise. We gathered the bundles and took them to Security where the letter was read and the food was distributed, with laughter and tears, eating cashews, prunes, chocolate, and ham—it was the first fresh food we had seen in a long time. As we walked back to our bunker to sack out, we heard shots from the APCs on the surrounding hills. Apparently they thought the bundles contained rifles and ammo so they broke the cease-fire and started a firefight. All around us bullets were hitting the ground and we flattened. ... That firefight lasted all day (Anderson, Brown, Lerner, and Shafer 1974: 176–77).

During the firefight a man named Frank Clearwater was hit in the head by a bullet that ripped through the wall of the church. His wife, Morningstar Clearwater, recounted:

> I was in Wounded Knee when my husband got shot—I had
> gone to get some food at the church. He was at the little
> white church, laying down on a mattress. And the shot
> came on the right hand side of the big white church and
> the next thing I knowed, my husband was shot in the head,
> laying on the mattress, and he was almost dead (Anderson,
> Brown, Lerner, and Shafer 1974: 176–77).

None of this, however, was covered directly on the nightly network news. News personnel were instead given information at a
government press conference in Pine Ridge that the firefight was
sparked by Wounded Knee occupants' unprovoked gunfire at an
FBI helicopter that had gone to inspect the occupation site after
the airdrop [10]. The government's exclusion of the press from
the scene of the event in question, of course, made it impossible
for reporters to have known exactly what happened.

Although the White House early on established a policy of
restraint, the FBI adopted a more aggressive stance toward the
occupation from the beginning. Consistent with the geopolitical
lens through which it had historically viewed such dissent, the
FBI understood Wounded Knee in particularly stark terms, arguing that "the problem at Wounded Knee is a military one which
requires a military solution" (SAC Minneapolis 1973: 3). A
12 March memo reported that the four SACs at Wounded Knee
"unanimously urge that the U.S. Army put down the insurrection
immediately since not equipped or trained to invade an armed
community" (Gebhardt 1973b). Further, without "such action
being taken by Federal Government," the FBI believed, "other
takeovers throughout the U.S. will logically result."

The FBI thus strongly pushed for deployment of the U.S.
Army's Domestic Disturbance Plan, code-named "Operation
Garden Plot." Like the *H. Rap Brown Act*, Garden Plot had been
drafted in 1968 to contain urban unrest. The plan specified
general strategies such as the deployment of large numbers of
troops, a focus on protecting life rather than property, and the
establishment of curfews that allowed for the easy identification
and control of deviant citizens and rabble-rousers. Garden Plot

also included specific plans targeted to each prospective trouble spot (*U.S. News & World Report* 1968). Military planners based these plans on detailed on-the-scene geographic research. Given the context out of which the plan emerged, it is no surprise that the focus was squarely on urban America. The first deployment of the plan, however, was not in the spaces for which it was intended—Los Angeles, Detroit, Newark—but in a decidedly marginal space. Wounded Knee, suffice it to say, was not the subject of advance military research and planning.

Upon news of the occupation, the White House triggered the plan. A division of the Army was put on alert, and an advisor was sent to Wounded Knee to make a firsthand evaluation of the scene. The person responsible for military advising at Wounded Knee and for assessing potential military involvement in the incident was Colonel Volney Warner, the Chief of Staff of the Army's 82nd Airborne Division. Based on this evaluation, he was to report a recommendation back to Washington. His assessment of the situation was unequivocal: strongly urging against deployment of military troops based on his belief that, *contra* FBI arguments, the occupation represented no threat to national security. In his view, it essentially constituted a local, if quite public, law enforcement issue. A then-classified memo explained:

> The name of the game is not to kill or injure the Indians. An Army involvement resulting in loss of life and injury would reflect badly on the Army. ... Because of the isolated geographical location, the seizure and holding of Wounded Knee poses no threat to the nation ... [though] it is conceded that this act is a source of irritation if not embarrassment to the Administration in general and the Department of Justice in particular (*New York Times* 1975).

Army observers at the scene—discreetly dressed, per explicit instructions, in civilian clothes to avoid drawing attention to the military's presence at the site of a domestic disorder—were extremely reluctant to dedicate their troops, in what would be a very *public* show of force.

Despite the pleading of senior FBI officials, the politics of deploying the military within domestic space were precarious. The *Posse Comitatus Act*, passed in 1878, had long set strict boundaries on the deployment of the military in domestic space. In his later memoirs, Felt (1979: 268) recounted a phone conversation with Attorney General Kleindienst about using Army troops. "The White House," Kleindienst explained to Felt, "wants to low-key this incident and there's no way we are going to use the Army." Military troops could only be deployed at the explicit request of the President or the Congress. As potentially problematic as such deployment was *anywhere* in the U.S., it was even more so given that the space in question was the subject of political controversy precisely over the nature and status of sovereignty. Deploying federal troops in the ambiguous, quasi-sovereign nations of Native America was thus a rather delicate proposition, a point that Army and White House officials were well aware of.

Although military involvement at Wounded Knee appears to have *restrained* the use of force, it did so in complex ways. On 28 March, military advisor Colonel Warner contacted the Attorney General's office in Washington with his proposed battle plan to forcibly retake Wounded Knee. Because of his continued argument against involvement of military troops, Warner's proposed plan specified the use of Marshal and FBI personnel. Instead of tangibly and publicly dedicating its troops, the Army quietly provided both tactical and logistical support, as well as hardware and supplies to the FBI, Marshal, and BIA personnel at Wounded Knee [11]. Kleindienst, however, refused to approve the plan, explaining "he did not want another Kent State" (Bates 1973).

While Kleindienst rejected the plan to retake Wounded Knee, the area around the site remained heavily militarized. Later trials revealed that during the occupation the Army furnished 16 APCs, 400,000 rounds of ammunition, 100 protective vests, one reconnaissance fighter, three helicopters, 120 sniper rifles, and 20 grenade launchers (Garbus 1974). This equipment was transported to the reservation by military vehicles, then "dropped off at various points miles away from Wounded Knee, transferred to civilian vehicles and then driven to the scene of battle by military men wearing civilian clothes" (Garbus 1974: 454).

The result was predictable. Throughout April, in particular, Wounded Knee was subject to increasingly intense fire from federal positions. As Vietnam veteran and Wounded Knee participant Roger Ironcloud put it, "We took more bullets in 71 days than I took in two years in Vietnam" (Garbus 1974: 454). Another Vietnam veteran at Wounded Knee suggested more concrete parallels with Vietnam (Anderson, Brown, Lerner, and Shafer 1974: 195):

> All you have to do is look around the hills here and you can see about 12 armored personnel carriers that are nothing but APCs that didn't make it to Vietnam. The men carry the same weapons that are used in Vietnam: The M-16, the M-79 grenade launcher is here, they have starlight scopes that were used for spotting people in the jungle at night time, they have infra-red sensors, trip flares out here in the woods to prevent our foot patrols from coming in. They use helicopters. So the similarities are more than just obvious.

And as public a war as Vietnam was, he continued, it also had aspects that were deliberately sheltered from public scrutiny. "Some of us," he explained, "went into Laos in civilian clothes to do operations of a military nature for the CIA. And we always hid from the American public and the press what was going on" (Anderson, Brown, Lerner, and Shafer 1974: 196).

Dimming the Media Spotlight and Concluding the Occupation

By late April, officials again discussed use of force. On 22 April, Deputy Assistant Attorney General Hellstern (1973) sent a memo to his superiors in Washington, urging a "police action" to forcibly regain control of Wounded Knee. Among his reasons for urging the action was an assessment of geographies of scale and of publicity. First, Hellstern noted the changing composition of occupiers and that this also changed the identity issues at stake in the occupation:

> The occupants of Wounded Knee are now composed of about 85 whites and 85 Indians. Very few regular residents remain. Therefore, the justification for restraint, particularly in terms of the aggrieved local populace, is no longer a real factor (1973: 2).

Wounded Knee now consisted largely of outsiders, which Hellstern seemed to be arguing would make aggressive action more acceptable to "the public." Closely tied to this was a second point about Pine Ridge power and authority:

> If the Government does not move quickly, we are going to encounter very real problems in dealing with white ranchers, the dispossessees of Wounded Knee, and others on the Reservation who want the confrontation ended. We may end up fighting the wrong people (Hellstern 1973: 2).

Finally, Hellstern noted two other important factors relating to the issue of containment and publicity. First, because of the exclusion of the media from the site, "[v]ery little press is out here now and a police action would have very little on-the-scene coverage" (1973: 2). Second, in Hellstern's view, it was the right time to move because college students were still in school:

> The Government should not only move before the college year is up, but should move quickly enough to stabilize the Reservation in the aftermath of the elimination of Wounded Knee before the college year is up. This is the only way to avoid real summer problems at Pine Ridge (1973: 2).

For all of these reasons, Hellstern advised aggressive action.

In the last week of April, officials laid plans for the forceful end of the occupation. On 25 April, Colburn (1973) explained to Sneed that Colonel Warner had informed him that "all items requested from the Department of Defense in support of my plan to seize Wounded Knee are now pre-positioned at Ft. Carson, Colorado, and can arrive at Pine Ridge six hours after notification." Should the decision be made to retake Wounded Knee, government forces were ready. Nevertheless, he continued, "[i]n view of recent White House guidance, execution of the plan does not appear imminent." Colonel Warner's battle plan to forcibly retake Wounded Knee was subsequently leaked to the press and outlined in a *New York Times* story on 30 April. The story described the plan as a part of a broader "last ditch effort to end the confrontation without further violence" (*New York Times* 1973). If negotiations failed, a government source reported, the Army's plan would be utilized. Consistent with the plan Warner had proposed in late March, military troops would not be used. Instead the Army would provide Marshals with necessary hardware and support [12]. To prepare for deployment of the plan, the Justice Department brought in more Marshals, while the Army provided additional ammunition and supplies and an armored helicopter that was equipped to flood the Wounded Knee site with tear gas (*New York Times* 1973). Importantly, however, there was no mention in the story of Colonel Warner himself, and the only explicit reference to the military was to the Army helicopter.

Although the 17 April airdrop had provided the occupiers with desperately needed food and supplies, they could hardly last forever. On 25 April, Frank Clearwater died. The next day, federal forces barraged Wounded Knee with what until then had been an unprecedented amount of government firepower: tear gas and flares, and thousands of rounds of ammunition. A number of occupiers were injured in the firefight, some seriously. Additionally, another man, Buddy Lamont, was killed by a bullet the next morning.

These latest events effectively ended the occupation. There was "a new seriousness after Buddy's death," a reporter from the alternative press wrote in her journal:

> Food's very short—most of the cooking is done outside now. The electricity was shot out during the firefight, so no lights and no running water. We're using kerosene lamps and hauling water from the old windmill (Anderson, Brown, Lerner, and Shafer 1974: 222).

Lamont's death, Dewing (1995: 120) summarizes, "marked the end of armed resistance and initiated negotiations that finally achieved a settlement." The occupation site was now so tightly contained that the firefight and its aftermath were left undocumented by the major television networks, and Lamont's death "barely found its way into the news" (Dewing 1995: 120).

The occupation ended, finally, on 8 May, with a whimper more than a bang. The NBC news reporter who announced the occupation's close that night did so, in fact, from a vantage point quite far in the distance. As he explained, media personnel remained barred from the site. At a press conference on the same day, Hellstern explained to these reporters the end of the occupation:

> The environment down in Wounded Knee has changed substantially in the last three weeks. We've made a concerted effort to really isolate the community down there from the outside world.

Such isolation included not just people, food, and supplies, but also the media that brought the event to distant publics. Indeed, the spectacle of Wounded Knee was quite effectively—violently even—contained.

Dissent and the Boundaries of Power and Resistance

The state's intensified—and increasingly violent—containment of the Wounded Knee site successfully brought the occupation to a close a short time later, on 8 May. The contested nature of power and authority over the space of the reservation and its relationship to the U.S. nation-state during the course of the Wounded Knee occupation was reflected in an equally complicated set of concrete boundary contests. In large part these contests revolved around the question of who had access to what spaces and on what terms. Such access was regulated through various kinds of boundaries. We can see this clearly in the various roadblocks and bunkers that different actors erected to regulate the space of the conflict. Both federal forces and the Wounded Knee occupiers themselves sought to effect control over the occupation through these concrete spatial tactics. AIM's efforts to reassert a more radical notion of sovereignty—to harden the line that defined the reservation itself—were also dependent on tactics that blurred that line in practice. Their use of the media is one example of how their claims to Wounded Knee were dependent on larger connections. By seizing this site and using it to project their claims widely and to make the occupation intensely public, the Wounded Knee occupiers hoped to press the state both into restraint and also toward some measure of agreement regarding their demands.

Together the occupiers and federal forces served to create what Deputy Attorney General Sneed referred to as a "protest platform." The occupation presented federal representatives with a new kind of political crisis in the Wounded Knee occupation. Sneed's decision to remove the federal roadblocks on 10 March and the occupiers' subsequent declaration of an independent state shows that the status of these boundaries was fluid. The removal of the federal roadblocks was recognition of the unique circumstances of this highly mediated protest event. The declaration of the ION was a similar recognition on the part of AIM leadership of the relationship between a politics of symbols and their grounding in the concrete boundaries that defined the spatial form of the occupation. Although it seems unlikely the occupiers had any real hope of creating an independent state, the move had the dramatic effect one would expect by raising before the public the centrality of treaty rights to the conflict and the inseparable issue of boundaries. Far from dissolving the boundary that defined the occupation site, in other words, the removal of the federal roadblocks resulted in the reinforcement of this boundary.

Wilson's tribal government was clearly unhappy with the ongoing status of this "protest platform" and wanted to use force to dissolve it. Frustrated with the restraint demanded by Washington, and enraged by the decision of an off-reservation federal judge to usurp his authority, Wilson instead asserted tribal sovereignty and established a roadblock of his own in direct defiance of the federal government. How federal officials responded to Wilson's defiance of their authority sheds interesting light on the internal dynamics of the state as they were expressed at Wounded Knee. Although FBI officials like Felt were charged with carrying out orders from above, they were often unhappy with these orders. Politically, key FBI decision-makers both in Washington and on the scene in South Dakota were more sympathetic to the aggressive position of Wilson. They were also occasionally engaged in their own bureaucratic conflicts with the U.S. Marshals. For whatever reason, the FBI ultimately refused to forcibly dismantle the tribal roadblock, and in so doing offered tacit support for it.

If Wounded Knee was a mediated spectacle, then, it was also much more than that. In part the Wounded Knee occupation dramatized a larger story about American Indian identity and its relation to American nationalism. The diverse practices by which different actors asserted their authority over this contested site also tells a story about the politics of sovereignty itself and how it is given shape through boundaries. Indigenous sovereignty claims sit in uneasy tension with dominant state-centered normative orders.

5

Elián González and the Geopolitics of Home

In 2000, South Florida was ground zero for the most bizarre of political spectacles. The presidential election in November saw the unprecedented occasion of an electoral limbo so bitterly contested that it took the Supreme Court to intervene, as partisans fought over "hanging chads" and ballot recounts. It also saw the Republican party using the tactics of confrontational protest politics to press their claims. As bizarre as the Florida election was, however, the battle over Elián González was stranger still, though no less instructive of the contentiousness of U.S. politics at the dawn of the 21st century. At one level the story was simple enough: A mother and child are traveling in a boat that capsizes in a storm. Stranded at sea, the mother is claimed by the ocean, while the child survives long enough to be rescued by a passing fishing boat, on a national holiday (Thanksgiving Day) no less. It would seem quite obvious, based on these simple facts, that the child would be reunited with his surviving parent: his father.

As Attorney General Janet Reno later put it, "The law is very clear. Clearly, a child who has lost his mother belongs with his sole surviving parent" (2000).

Life is rarely so simple, however. For what immediately became the issue was the geographic story here: that the mother and child were crossing not just any expanse of water, but the 90 miles between Cuba and the United States. At some point, then, they crossed a threshold, into that ambiguous twilight zone where everyday notions of time and space do not hold: 1999 could have just as easily been 1969, with conservatives quickly attempting to reinstate the clean logics of Cold War geopolitical distinctions and to place the boy firmly on the side of freedom, justice, and the "American way." One commentator described the spectacle surrounding the boy as "a weird cross between a Cold War showdown and a soap opera, the Bay of Pigs Meets *All My Children*" (*Newsweek* 2000a). Lines were drawn between good and evil, as well as us and them, certainly, but also quite literally with respect to the "here" and "there" of a geographic morality play.

The case of Elián González conjured up age-old ghosts of Cuban political battles. For the Miami Cuban Right, the issues at stake were sharply divided into freedom and totalitarianism. To return the child to Cuba was not only to consign him to the tyranny of a communist state, but in so doing to contribute to its survival by validating it as a legitimate member of the community of states. Yet the broad contours of the geopolitical discourses of the Miami Cuban community were refracted through two further discourses. On one hand, the international orientation of the conflict intersected with a domestic discourse about the tyrannical federal state. This theme in turn resonated with the mainstream American Right, who saw in the incident yet another example of an overaggressive state trampling on the freedom to dissent.

There has been much written about the case, but my interest in this chapter is with its spatial inflection. My focus is on how the conflict over Elián was played out in and between three primary spaces. First, I analyze the abstract space of law. Here my interest is in how the legal aspect of the conflict centered on discourses of citizenship and a politics of boundaries. How, put simply, did the two sides in the conflict justify their arguments about what place the boy should call home? I then turn to Miami to examine how the conflict played out in the city's public spaces. Again, we return to the themes of the intersection of a politics of citizenship and a politics of space. Finally, I examine how the very public spectacle of the case was also tied to the private spaces of the home where Elián stayed. Indeed, much of the public spectacle played out in and around the private space of the home. How, then, did the home serve as site around which all of these questions swirled?

Child or Citizen?
The Book

On either side of the Florida Straits, the politics of the Elián case revolved around stark Cold War discourses that opposed good from evil, freedom from tyranny, the nurturing family from the dominance of the state. Beneath these grand discourses, however, one finds familiar themes of citizenship, identity, and space. In the remainder of this chapter, I first analyze the legal debates that swirled around the Elián case and then move on to how these were played out in various spaces.

The legal debate pitted those who appealed to the uniformity of the rule of law against those who sought to bend it to the exigencies of geopolitical context. Liberal law is based on an abstract notion of citizenship that regularizes rights and duties across individuals and across space. The citizen enshrined in law, however, is not just any subject. Law has historically made all manner of exceptions to the law of equivalence on which it is based. In the United States, blacks could not vote until the 19th century, and women not until the 20th century. Gays and lesbians still fail to enjoy the legal benefits of straight married couples: medical benefits, the right to make life-and-death medical decisions, and so forth.

Law also serves to constitute identity and citizenship around three further issues of relevance to the case of Elián González. The first is age. Children are yet another category of less-than-citizen, with restrictions on their capacity to exercise the duties and rights of citizenship. Children are unable to vote. They are restricted in their ability to move across space. They cannot operate motor vehicles or travel across geopolitical boundaries unaccompanied by a parent, except in rare instances. They are likewise restricted in their capacity to occupy—via age-specific curfews—public spaces at particular times. Their bodies are also carefully regulated. They are forbidden from consuming otherwise legal mind-altering substances like alcohol. The general rules that structure the formal definition of citizenship in essence amount to a presumption of an individual—generalized into an abstract legal subject—with the capacity to fulfill the duties and responsibilities of citizenship. Above all, they must be fully capable of independent judgment and possess an awareness of individual responsibility and culpability. A child's status as less-than-citizen is based precisely on its presumed inability to match these standards.

Second, the definition of the citizenship status of a child is wrapped up in larger definitions of family. Alessia Bell argues that "the child . . . is the raison d'être of family. Contemporary law knows this" (2001). She argues the rights claims of parenting have traditionally been divided by what she calls "blood, state, and sweat." Parental rights have historically been most strongly based on biological blood, in turn connected to patriarchal property rights. The 20th century saw a greater relative shift away from property toward a focus on the labor of child-rearing, and thus toward motherhood. At the same time, the relative de-biologicizing of parental rights in the contemporary era means that rights are often open to greater interpretation. Consider, for example, the meaning of blood in contexts such as surrogate motherhood, gay and lesbian families, and *in vitro* fertilization. In addition, the greater role of states in managing social reproduction has increasingly placed them in the role of both defining parental rights and (in some cases) fulfilling them. If a child is deemed to lack the capacity for sound independent judgment, then who is it that stands in to represent that child's "best interests"? A biological parent? An extended family member? Or perhaps in the absence of a clearly competent family member, the state itself?

The final issue of relevance in the Elián case was the boy's status as an illegal immigrant; yet another category of less-than-citizen that placed him outside the boundaries of law and thus of formal citizenship. The peculiar nature of U.S. immigration policies with respect to Cuba—which I discuss more below—offer greater opportunities for otherwise illegal immigrants who manage to make it ashore. Yet Elián did not. As such, beyond being a minor with a surviving parent, the boy's immigration status was such that under virtually any normal circumstances, he would have been immediately returned to his country of origin. Because he had no formal immigration status in the United States—he was in essence a nonperson from the standpoint of the law—he had no real basis to stay in Miami.

The formal legal debate about whether Elián should return to Cuba thus involved all of these aspects of the boy's identity before the law and centered on three questions. First, did the boy have any legitimate abstract claim to asylum? This question was about his immigration status. Second, if yes, did he—as a child—have any right to petition for asylum? This centered on his citizenship status with respect to age. Finally, if Elián himself could not speak before the law, who could present his case in his stead? This last question related to how the law distributed familial rights. All of these questions were essential to answering the more fundamental question: Where should Elián call home?

The extended family repeatedly asserted the boy's right to citizenship. All of their efforts thus centered on this issue. The asylum claim meant to establish a legal presence in the United States apart from the father in Cuba. To do that, they claimed, first, that the boy had legitimate fear of persecution if he were to return to Cuba. The legal argument centered on this issue. Second, they argued that because the surviving parent was subject to the same persecution, his statements on his wishes for Elián could not be taken at face value. Therefore, the child's stated wishes should trump those of his father's. Finally, the Miami family argued that in the absence of legal recognition of Elián's capacity for sound judgment, they should be allowed to represent his interests before the law.

Yet the law recognized none of these claims. The child himself had no legal right to petition for asylum. As Deputy Attorney General Eric Holder later put it, "At the core of this case is a little boy—so young that he does not have the capacity to make legal decisions for himself" (2000). Likewise, an INS decision memorandum concluded that "[a]t his tender age, Elián does not have the capacity to seek asylum on his own behalf" (Cooper 2000). The child—*as* a child—had less-than-full rights to citizenship quite apart from his immigration status.

Likewise, the extended family had no right to file the petition on his behalf given the surviving father. International immigration law typically applies standards of custody and family not of the country of destination, but of the country of origin. This is precisely to help mitigate the potential for international custody disputes, in which extranational states become wrapped up in adjudicating. The greater freedom of movement afforded by contemporary transportation systems, *and* the simultaneous durability of international boundaries and the legal territories they delineate, heightens the potential for international conflicts over child custody. States are thus loath to issue rulings that directly contradict standard custody policies of a child's country of origin. And as the INS noted, "Cuban law . . . reinforces the right of both parents to exercise parental authority" (Cooper 2000). Legal precedent thus held that father's rights trumped all.

When the INS formally announced its decision on the Elián case, it couched it in a language of the objective rule of law. As INS Commissioner Doris Meissner put it,

> This decision has been based on the facts and the law. Both U.S. and international law recognize the unique relationship between parent and child, and family reunification has long been a cornerstone of both American immigration law and INS practice. ... We urge everyone involved to understand, respect, and uphold the bond between parent and child and the laws of the United States (2000).

Likewise, a State Department spokesman also emphasized the rationality and generality of law as it would be applied in the case of Elián:

> This case will be followed according to normal procedures. It has nothing to do with Cuba as such. There are no special procedures. It will be followed according to the book (*The Miami Herald* 1999a).

The position of government officials was thus both that the law was unambiguous and that it placed authority for decisions relating to the boy in the hands of the father.

"Family Values" and the Politics of Scale

If administration officials appealed to the rule of an objective and dispassionate law as rooted in legal precedent, those that supported keeping Elián in Miami responded by asserting that legal precedent was of little use when applied to Cuba. For them, to measure the rights of a boy fleeing tyranny against those of a father subject to it was comparing apples to oranges. One lawyer in the keep-the-boy-in-Miami camp asked, "Which kind of a family is a less important factor in how this boy should be raised than which kind of state" (*Time* 2000a). Conservative columnist George F. Will, meanwhile, drew on an almost poststructuralist sensibility in arguing:

> Children need fathers, but they need the culture of freedom even more. To assume that Elián's father has an indefeasible right to immerse Elián in Cuba's highly ideologized tyranny . . . is to make a fetish of biology (2000).

A similar point was echoed in a protest sign outside the Little Havana house where the boy stayed that read, "Freedom Supercedes Fatherhood" (*Time* 2000b).

Conceptions of family were thus central to the legal battle and to the broader conflict over whether the boy would return to Cuba or stay in Miami. This accounts in large part for why the case resonated with a broader conservative American public and its discourses of family values and freedom. Amid the heightened political climate of a presidential campaign season, Republican candidates had no shortage of public comments on the matter. Senator John McCain argued during a debate that Elián should stay because "his mother sacrificed her life in order that her son could have freedom," and Steve Forbes called Elián "Bill Clinton's human sacrifice to Fidel Castro" (*The Miami Herald* 2000a), conjuring up images of a corrupt and amoral political leader feeding a child to an ogre.

Here, then, the issue revolved around the relationship between family, state, and child. For those who wanted to keep Elián in Miami, the boy's father could not fulfill the duties of citizenship required of a parent not because he was a poor father—indeed, at one point a lawyer working with the Miami family said that "[o]ur position is not that the father is a bad guy" (*The Miami Herald* 1999a)—but rather because he lived in Cuba. Under the conditions imposed by the Castro regime, the father lacked the free will necessary for sound judgment and action. Therefore, in balancing different rights claims with respect to family and to residence, they argued, the courts ought to consider the international geopolitics of human rights.

Conservatives thus sought to both loosen and expand the tightly drawn boundaries of belonging and identity that are typically associated with the conservative discourses of family. Conservative politics of boundaries and belonging have long held in some tension the micro-geographies of family and home, on one hand, and the macro-geographies of nationalism. "Family values" involves not so much a private sphere wholly sheltered from the public world of the state as a discourse about the relation between the private and the public; about making a particular story of the American family a story of the American nation-state as a whole. Will's disparagement of the "fetish of biology" he associated with those who argued the father's rights trumped all is thus perhaps less of a contradiction to conservative discourses of family and state than it appears on face value. By loosening the bounds of family in this circumstance, they sought to harden the boundaries of the nation itself vis-à-vis Cuba. For them, the larger context of citizenship as shaped by state practices was—at least in these rather strategically political discourses—more important than the bonds of blood in the equation of where the boy ought to live.

Even Republicans were split on the issue of how to adjudicate the conflicting claims, however. Senator Orrin Hatch argued, "When it comes to this little Cuban boy, there is only one concern that everybody ought to have in their minds, and that is what is in the best interest of that child. We have laws in this country that will basically take care of those interests" (*The Miami Herald* 2000a). Still, this left rather unanswered the question of *which* institution in fact best represented the law in this case. Some, like then-presidential-candidate Al Gore, argued the courts represented the ultimate authority over the questions at issue. "[T]he ultimate decision as to what is in this boy's best interest should be made on the basis of the rule of law according to due process—not politics and not diplomacy," Gore said in a statement, and "[t]he courts are in the best position to make this determination" (*The Miami Herald* 2000a).

In all the legal challenges, courts upheld the reasonableness of the federal government's response. Still, in rejecting the extended family's appeal, the Federal District Court in Florida did express concern—that echoed in part Will's position—about the degree to which law's smooth surface extended beyond borders:

> According to the INS policy, that a parent lives in a communist-totalitarian state is no special circumstance, sufficient in and of itself, to justify the consideration of a 6-year-old child's asylum claim (presented by a relative in this country) against the wishes of the nonresident parent. We acknowledge, as a widely accepted truth, that Cuba does violate human rights and fundamental freedoms and does not guarantee the rule of law to people living in Cuba. . . . Persons living in such a totalitarian state may be unable to assert freely their own legal rights, much less the legal rights of others. Moreover, some reasonable people

> might say that a child in the United States inherently has a substantial conflict of interest with a parent residing in a totalitarian state when that parent—even when he is not coerced—demands that the child leave this country to return to a country with little respect for human rights and basic freedoms (*González v. Reno et al.* 2000).

Seeming to open the door to a divergence from legal precedent, the court suggested that parental rights were not sacrosanct and that geopolitical considerations ought to provide some weight in INS decisions.

Critics of the decision emphasized the notable lack of ambiguity of the citizenship status of children before the law. "A child can't go to the dentist without permission, can't have any kind of emergency surgery, can't choose school, religion, clothing, housing," noted one expert in children's law, suggesting that if "you took this ruling to its logical extension, a child would have the right to go to court and say, 'I'm a New Yorker, but I want to move to California'" (*Time* 2000c). Another lawyer—this one specializing in immigration law—characterized the court's opinion as hinting at the potential for a "rather dramatic departure from the law" and argued that "Elián is a little kid, and only in a surrealistic world can you argue that he is making the asylum decision himself" (*U.S. News & World Report* 2000). Still another asked rhetorically, "Does this mean lawyers can hang out at the gates of Disney World as families depart and children cry out, 'I don't want to go!'?"

The citizenship questions opened up in the case were not only drawn around age and the geopolitical status of Cuba within a global human rights regime, but also how these issues intersected around the politics of immigration. Some immigrant rights activists noted that Elián was but one of thousands of children in broadly similar circumstances. And yet, they argued, the child from Cuba received the most intense interest from media and the political establishment, while other children did not. One Miami activist held a rally to dramatize the unique status of Cuban refugees in U.S. immigration policy to the detriment of others. As he explained, "This is the country of opportunity for everybody.

The little Cuban Elián González came here and we opened our hearts, but I don't see that happening with the Haitian people" (*The Miami Herald* 2000b).

The unique circumstances of the immigration status of Elián were in fact part of a larger pattern of state practices and policies that shaped movement across the Florida Straits. The U.S. Congress formalized an exceptional status for Cuban immigrants with its passage of the *Cuban Adjustment Act* in 1966. The act stipulated that any Cuban migrant who arrived in the United States and managed to stay for a period of 1 year could petition for residency status. U.S. immigration law in essence encouraged illegal Cuban migration by opening an interpretive gap that separated legitimate residency claims from illegitimate, all of which applied specifically to migrants from Cuba.

In the 1990s, the Clinton administration sought to close that gap slightly by removing the 1-year stay requirement. All migrants intercepted at sea were to be returned to Cuba, while all making it ashore could petition to remain in the United States. In seeking to resolve ambiguities, however, the so-called "wet feet, dry feet" policy arguably served to heighten them. For example, Guantánamo Bay—that geopolitical purgatory so central to the contemporary War on Terror—also became a site of similar controversy over the ambiguity of its territoriality with respect to the new immigration policies. Under the new policy, when the U.S. Coast Guard intercepted migrants at sea, they moved them to Guantánamo before repatriation. Yet, some of the migrants argued, the base was in effect U.S. territory and thus their feet were dry with respect to the new policy. That there might emerge a specific case that reflected the more general ambiguity of U.S. immigration policy with respect to Cuba was almost certain.

La Lucha y La Calle: Public Space and Community Identity
Two Cubas

Many of the stories in this book are about movement and settlement, belonging and estrangement. They involve issues, in other words, of how identity is tied to place. To understand the unique spectacle of the Elián González case—and why it was instantly about much more than abstract legal debates—it must be placed before the backdrop of the previous 4 decades of the historical geography of Cuban nationhood. Split by the politics of revolution and reaction, as well as by geography, Cuba in essence consists of two nations separated by the Florida Straits. On one side lie the champions of anti-imperialist nationalism and antibourgeois revolution. On the other lie the true believers in the moral rightness of democratic capitalism as led by the United States.

Within this context the Miami Cuban community is a collective identity of "outsiders" of a unique sort. From the standpoint of Anglo-America, the community is but one of a myriad of immigrant communities, marked by differences of language and culture, and bound together by a shared past and connection to place. Yet the Miami Cuban community might be better understood less as an immigrant community that has left its nation behind—somewhere else and in the past—than a community in exile oriented toward the future of the country they left.

In his interpretation of the identity politics surrounding constructions of the exile community and how the Elián González case activated it in uniquely charged ways, Miguel De La Torre (2003) argues that the mythic Cuba at the center of exile identity represents a merging of political ideology, place, and religious fervor. The hegemonic Cuban exile identity is one of a deep conservatism rooted in the certainties of a religious worldview and a politics of unwavering absolutes. The fall of Batista and the rise of Castro in 1959 represents a line drawn in time that sharply divides a period of idealized nationhood from the fall from grace that followed. From one perspective, then, the politics of exile nationhood are profoundly nostalgic: rooted in a mythic past. In one of his two books on Miami, David Rieff recounts the story of a Cuban professional living in New York, who said of Little Havana:

> As you walk down Eighth Street, in a sense you have entered a time capsule that has transported you to the

past. In Miami Cubans live or try to live *La Cuba de ayer,* the Cuba of yesterday. It is a mythical country we fabricated, where nostalgia and myth abound (1987: 152).

La Cuba de ayer is thus central to contemporary exile nationalism. In this vision, the Cuba of yesterday is socially cohesive, politically free, geographically intact.

Yet the politics of exile nationalism is not solely retrospective. Instead, the historical imagery at once reflects a contest for the future of Cuba and accounts for the peculiar politics of the community. It involves, as De La Torre writes, "a (re)invention of a community's vision of itself that is both religious and future-oriented" (2003). The time of exile since the Revolution is seen as an ongoing struggle—referred to as *La Lucha* [13]—to save the nation from the tyranny of a communist dictatorship. Everything is refracted through the lens of that struggle: work, religion, family, and, perhaps most intensely, politics and ideology.

The political teleology of exile nationalism accounts in part for its intensity. De La Torre (2003) goes so far as to call the politics of *La Lucha* against the Castro regime a "Holy War." *La Lucha,* he argues, represents

> a cosmic struggle between the children of light (Exilic Cubans) and the children of darkness (Resident Cubans), complete with a Christ (Marti), an Antichrist (Castro), a priesthood (CANF), a promised land (Cuba), and martyrs (those who gloriously suffer in the Holy War against Castro). Add to this cosmology a messiah—Elián (2003).

The exile model citizen at the center of the dominant Miami Cuban identity is constructed, according to De La Torre, as a white, relatively prosperous, aggressively masculinist, homophobic man. This dominant construction of Cubanness is rooted in a historical perspective that distinguishes an earlier wave of migrants from the more recent period that began with the Mariel boatlift and which has been characterized as largely nonwhite. In this sense, De La Torre argues, the model citizen at the heart of dominant constructions of Miami Cuban identity is paradoxically racist. In asserting the myth of a predominantly white nation, this perspective erases the reality of a biracial nation, reflecting what Goldberg (2002) refers to as a "raceless" identity politics that in claiming to be beyond race, actually reinforces it.

The conflicts over the identity politics of the community have always been aggressive and often turned violent. In the 1970s and 1980s, Miami was wracked by a series of what can only be described as political assassinations. Public figures who challenged the hard-line anti-Castro orthodoxy of the Miami Cuban community—many of them in the media—were common victims. In a three-year period in the 1970s, anti-Castro groups engaged in over 100 politically motivated attacks in South Florida (Bardach 2002). The violence peaked in the 1980s, as political groups bombed a whole series of buildings; from businesses to foreign consulates, all seen as representing the betrayals of collaboration with the Castro regime.

In 1986, the South Florida Peace Coalition held a demonstration protesting U.S. aid to the Nicaraguan Contras. The issue was a divisive one throughout the country, but no place more so than in Miami, where the Cuban community saw it not only as a reflection of an abstract contest over political ideology—the evils of communism against the salvation of "democracy"—but as a proxy battle between Castro's Cuba and Reagan's America. The presence of what radical anti-Castro groups like Alpha 66 saw as communist sympathizers agitating in an important Miami public space was, plainly put, intolerable.

The Elián González story is but one example of a larger struggle over the present and future standing of a Cuban nation intensely fractured both by politics and by geography. It fused together the symbolic politics of childhood innocence with the geopolitical contest over Cuban nationhood. The conflict, in turn, was played out in a variety of venues. Among them was the formal world of courtrooms and hearing chambers, ruled as they are by the rituals of bureaucracy and law. Equally important were the concrete public spaces of the city.

La Calle

The politics of Cubanness is worked out not only in the rituals of law and bureaucracy and the virtual spaces of the media, but also in the concrete spaces of the city. In this section, I explore how the struggle over the future of Cuba was manifest in the public spaces of Miami during the course of the Elián González saga and how this in turn intersected with the politics of mediated spectacle.

With the case of Elián González, leadership in both Cuban communities—the one in Cuba, and the one in Miami—quickly used the incident to marshal resources. These battles, of course, were never about legal abstractions alone, or even primarily. Indeed, conflict over Elián's legal status was a public spectacle from the very beginning. The two sides marshaled forces in both the concrete spaces of Miami and Havana and the virtual spaces of media. In so doing, they sought to constitute the public in their own image and so to shape to the conduct of affairs.

Shortly after the boy was recovered from the sea, Fidel Castro announced defiantly, "We will move heaven and earth to get the child back! If they have any brains, they will make sure the boy is returned within 72 hours." In an interview, Castro pointed to the battle over public opinion, and the importance of conjuring up strong publics with the capacity to influence the course of events, when he said, "I hope that Cuba's numerous friends in the United States and in other parts will begin to organize committees for the release of the child kidnapped by the United States. Heaven and earth will be moved" (*The Miami Herald* 1999b).

Each Cuba had its privileged symbolic sites. The regime immediately seized on the incident, staging massive protests on the streets of Havana and making intensive use of state-controlled media to marshal support both at home and abroad. The public spaces around the American Interest section of Havana was one important location in Cuba and a frequent site of dramatic public protests. And in what *The Miami Herald* referred to as an addition to "the orchestrated campaign of public fury" that characterized Cuba's response to the situation, an estimated "1,000 grandmothers marched through Cardenas in support of the boy's father" (*The Miami Herald* 1999c).

Perhaps most prominent, however, was the micro-space of Elián's schoolroom. Cuban television regularly ran images of the room and the students agonizing over the boy's absence. His desk sat empty, wrapped in a sign that read "untouchable," as if to dramatize the child's absence. Toward this end, Cuban television broadcast images from Elián's school, with crying colleagues pleading for his return, and the boy's empty school desk dramatizing his absence. Notably, although the schoolroom was a space symbolic of childhood innocence, it was also a public space of the state; not a domestic interior.

In Miami, by contrast, the drama focused on the private home of the extended family where Elián stayed for the duration of his time in Florida. Around this site, the public battle pitted the extended family against the federal state. The family represented the religiously inflected worldviews of the Miami Cuban community more broadly. The INS and the Department of Justice represented the abstractions of state-sanctioned law and with it the authority of the state itself.

In turn, the battle between these two perspectives was dramatized on a public stage: in the opinion pieces and letters to the editors of newspapers, in the brashly conservative commentary on Miami's radio airwaves, and on television news. Much of the public identity of the Miami Cuban community has been worked out through local media. Radio has played a particularly strong role. As Bardach characterizes it, "A good deal of Miami Spanish language radio has operated as the Big Brother of the community" (2002: 103). By this she means it is heavily politicized to the point of serving to enhance a hegemonic ideological perspective that not only is intolerant of dissent, but whose power of persuasion extends to the concrete politics of the streets. On more than one occasion, as just one example, the FCC has fined Miami radio stations for incitement to riot.

Newspapers have also been a battleground of sorts. The dominant ideological slant of the city's editorial pages has historically been consistent with that of hegemonic exile politics, and when papers have strayed from an anti-Castro position they have often suffered as a result. When, for example, *The Miami Herald* published an editorial in 1992 critical of efforts to tighten the sanctions against Cuba, the staunchly anti-Castro Cuban American National Foundation launched a high-profile public campaign to discredit the paper. The paper also found its vending machines vandalized and its publisher the victim of death threats (Levine 2000).

The case of Elián González as it played out in Miami was above all a political spectacle dramatized in the public spaces of the city and projected onto a mediated public sphere. Activists in the Miami Cuban community pressed their representation of the meaning of the event on the streets and in local media. Among the publics conjured by the Elián spectacle was the homegrown conservative in the Miami community. Yet the case also resonated more widely, with a larger national conservative movement.

A story in *The Miami Herald* commented on the degree to which media exposure seemed to influence not just the conduct of the legal battle, but how the conflict played out in the streets. The story described a scene where the night before police had cleared the area with tear gas. Before the local evening news broadcasts, the story noted, "no more than 80 people milled around two television trucks parked on a corner" (*The Miami Herald* 2000c). Within an hour, the scene dramatically changed:

> By 10 p.m., three more TV trucks had arrived and sprouted antennas. A helicopter hovered. The crowd had more than tripled. Police were lined up in riot gear. People were much more animated, as was the cacophony of chants and car horns. At 11 p.m., with most local stations broadcasting from the intersection, people hoisted posters not seen there all day; the crowd swelled even more. At midnight, almost a half-hour after the newscasts had ended, and 24 hours after the previous night's tear-gas confrontation, the corner was completely clear. No TV trucks. No protesters. No parked cars. Only the occasional police cruiser and curious motorist drove past.

Some in the exile community raised concerns. One of those in the crowd was 77-year-old Watergate burglar Eugenio Rolando Martinez. He was there, according to the reporter covering the story, to serve as a "moderating influence" on both police and protesters. "I shouldn't be saying it," he said, "but I believe that a lot of the trouble in the crowd is because of this," by which he meant the television cameras. "Some of these people," he argued, "don't even know why they're here." Miami Police spokesman Lt. Bill Schwartz concurred, arguing that "[p]eople who have a genuine concern and want to get their message out will use the television as a forum; people who just want to cause trouble and act silly will use television as an exhibitionist platform."

The question of how to dissent was one raised in the exile community from the beginning. Initially, activists made a point not to take to the streets, in part to distinguish themselves from the protests in Cuba, which they characterized as bellicose and a contrived political show. The no-protest period quickly evaporated amid the heated political conflict, but the theme of the need for respectable and principled dissent emerged in various contexts. Later in the saga, for example, a crowd of thousands protested outside the home where the boy was staying. Along with the intense media presence, singer Gloria Estefan came to lend support. She said the following before the crowd and the cameras:

> We are a peaceful community. We're asking all Cuban-Americans to continue protesting as they have done so far, in a respectful manner, and not be carried away into violence or civil disobedience (*The Miami Herald* 2000d).

In actions and rhetoric such as this, individuals like Estefan and Martinez sought to constitute the exile community as a public with common purpose and force of will, as well as to represent that community before a larger American public as morally committed and disciplined dissidents. They insisted on their rights to the streets as a necessary venue in which to dramatize legitimate dissent. At the same time, they sought to constitute the exile community—in essence, Elián's new family—as disciplined; fully respectful of the duties of citizenship.

Raul Martinez, then-mayor of Hialeah, FL, discussed the need to balance the right to dissent for one segment of his community against the right to peace for others. "We have to not look out for the right of one group, but for the rights of the entire community" (Olkon, Epstein Nieves, and Merzer 2000), he said. Moreover, he was concerned about the *appearance* of dissent before the media spotlight, speculating that "[w]hen this gets on national television, what sympathy is the rest of the country going to have?"

Still, the point bears repeating that community is not natural and organic, but constructed. Despite all the appearance of an unwaveringly unified position on all things Cuban, the Miami Cuban community is itself a discourse shaped by practices. As one exile put it, "When everyone talks about the Cuban exile community supporting this kid, what are they talking about? They may control the Spanish radio stations that try to manipulate everyone with their propaganda, but they don't represent the entire Cuban community in Miami" (Olkon, Epstein Nieves, and Merzer 2000).

The Politics of Home

Private Spaces

The most important site in Miami was the home of Lazaro González, where Elián stayed for the duration of his time in Florida. While the incident presented clear protagonists, and an easily drawn theme, both of which played well on the evening news, it also took place on a clearly defined stage. In the case of the little boy from Cuba, that stage proved to be the suburban house of Elián's uncle, where the boy stayed for the duration of his time in Miami (Figure 5.1). That house served as a metaphor for a larger drama. This fact became reflected in the protesters arrayed outside who—brandishing Cuban flags and Catholic symbols—vowed to

Fig. 5.1 Scene outside González home in Little Havana. (Photograph courtesy of AP/Wide World Photos, used by permission.)

protect Elián and his new home from the outside intrusion of the state and what many saw as its illegitimate intention to remove the boy and send him back to Cuba. The army of media personnel who covered this spectacle served to turn this drama into one of national, even global, import.

On one hand, the space around the home provided a platform on which to stage the spectacle. From the beginning, all of the symbolic presence of the Miami Cuban community seemed condensed into the space immediately outside this home. Supporters of the boy and his continued presence in Miami displayed signs, conducted prayer vigils, constructed shrines, played music, and vowed to protect the boy. Further, photographers and news camerapeople were on constant watch for daily appearances of the boy before the media spotlight.

The home, then, was a complexly mediated space of dissent. It offered a platform to both dramatize larger opposition to state authority, as well as provide the boundaries of shelter—largely symbolic—from the intrusion of unwanted bodies and the authority they represented. *The Miami Herald* described the scene inside and outside the home in the following way:

A world of politicians, lawyers, strategists and professional
Castro-haters has taken over the small two-bedroom house
where the child is living with his Miami relatives. An army
of photographers, cameramen, reporters, and technicians
has taken over the area surrounding the house (2000e).

"They have become prisoners in their own home," the story concluded, "a modest, beige stucco house in Miami's Little Havana."

The home is arguably the symbolic site par excellence of American nationalism. Within hegemonic national myth, the home is
the bounded space of the nuclear family, representing a private
sphere of individuals who share common blood and common
space. It is a space of reprieve from the public duties of work and
citizenship; a space of idealized family and nationhood. Feminists
have long challenged this perspective of the home as haven from
both work and the obligations of the state (Massey 1994), offering
a more complex view of the social production of domestic space
and of the dynamics of work and citizenship in which it is wrapped
up. The home from this perspective ranges from being viewed as at
worst a site of exploitation—a space where women have been historically bound—to a more ambivalent space: one both of exploitation and of nurturing, work as well as reprieve (hooks 1990).

So how, then, were discourses of home marshaled in the context of the Elián González case? One striking way focused on
how the home shaped the relationship between the boy and the
(extended) family. The very public spectacle that took place outside the modest suburban home revolved not only around the
grand geopolitical demons conjured up by the Miami Cuban population, but also, at the same time, around arguments about
domesticity. Beyond serving as a stage, the home also served to
mark off the private space of the domestic from the intensely public space of the spectacle outside and pointed to the deeply political, if often masked, nature of that distinction. The space behind
closed doors became at once intensely public, with debates by
media pundits about exactly what was taking place behind those
doors. Did the surrogate family provide a healthy environment
for the child? Did the boy's cousin provide the maternal figure

tragically lost and now so necessary to provide continuity? Or was the boy subject to psychological manipulation, caught up in the very public discourse of the Miami Cuban population?

Those who wanted to keep Elián in Miami argued that the family provided nurturing relationships important to the boy's well-being and thus that the home itself was a nurturing space. In this vision, the extended family in essence became recentered as the primary nurturers; as a kind of surrogate nuclear family. The discourse of the nurturing family thus became spatialized within the boundaries of the home.

This discourse in turn was couched in heavily gendered terms. Much of the discourse of the nurturing family home centered on Elián's cousin: a then-21-year-old woman named Marisleysis González. From the beginning, many portrayed the young woman as the maternal figure that sheltered the boy from both the grief of losing his mother, as well as the onslaught of the outside world. As she herself put it, "I know I have to be strong for Elián because I'm the mother figure in his life" (*The Miami Herald* 2000e).

Critics instead offered a very different perspective on the character of the family home. Rather than nurturing the child so as to allow his essential being freedom of expression, they argued instead that the extended family manipulated the child and his presence before the cameras to promote their own ideological perspective. Further, they charged that Marisleysis González was far from the nurturing maternal figure. Instead, they portrayed her as an unstable woman who exploited the child for her own ideological purposes, trotting him before media cameras to bring before the public images of the nurturing alternative to life in Cuba [14].

The height of the conflict over the meaning of home—sanctuary or prison—was manifest in the response to the airing in April of a late-night videotape of the child emphatically telling his father he wished to stay in Miami. For many, the video bordered on child abuse. "That video," said a medical ethicist, "was political kiddie porn. It's clearly exploitation" (*The Miami Herald* 2000f). The ethicist's point relied on an interpretation of the citizenship status of children vis-à-vis adults, as well as of the extended family vis-à-vis the surviving parent. In turn, he linked these concerns to an argument about the nature of media itself; saying that "[c]hildren are not competent to give their consent to be on TV. It never should have been taken. It never should have been broadcast." A Clinton administration official echoed the sentiment by saying, "This is the most appalling example so far of this child being manipulated and exploited by the Miami relatives who continue to block Elián's immediate reunification with his father" (*The Miami Herald* 2000f)

How the politics of identity and citizenship with the Elián case intersected around the home extended beyond its immediate and stable boundaries. The debates about the videotape were one example. Here the issue centered on how representation was mediated: how meaning was moved across the public/private divide. From the home-as-haven perspective, the videotape was a neutral bearer of the legitimate interests and desires of the child. For those who argued from the home-as-prison standpoint, the boundaries of the home shielded the family from legitimate public scrutiny. That shelter provided a space within which to organize representation to fulfill narrow ambitions that were at odds with the needs of the child.

Domestic Space and State Power

The question of how authority and meaning moved across the boundaries of the home—or not—was also evidenced in a much more high-profile example: how to enforce the state's will on the matter of where Elián should live. In particular, in the face of repeated refusals to turn over the child, should state force be applied to resolve the situation? Put differently, should the state hold out for the citizens' willing compliance with its authority and therefore the surrender of the child from the private space of the home to public world beyond? Or should it forcefully cross the boundary of the home to enforce its authority? If the question about Elián González was where the boy ought to call home, the question presented to authorities was where does the state properly reside?

The issue was highlighted, in quite dramatic fashion, by the response to the events of 22 April. By April, Justice Department officials were increasingly frustrated by the González family's refusal to hand over Elián, despite repeated legal and bureaucratic rulings that upheld his repatriation to Cuba and to his father. Lazaro González defiantly proclaimed, "They will have to take this child by force" (*Time* 2000d).

A *Newsweek* story described the scene around the home in the following way:

> As women in black dresses made prayer circles, burly men formed flying squads to crash the barricades. Pop diva Gloria Estefan held forth for the cameras, and movie star Andy Garcia asked to have his picture taken with the child (2000b).

The crowds around the home were increasingly large and aggressive; prepared to guard the home against any potential intrusion by federal forces. Federal officials pointed to a picture of a home surrounded by a dangerous group of people: bodyguards with concealed weapons permits, 15–20 men—many of them with violent criminal records—camped out in tents pitched in a neighbor's yard, and reported spottings by federal agents of members of the paramilitary group Alpha 66 (*Newsweek* 2000c). Likewise, local officials were publicly refusing to facilitate the removal of the boy.

As federal officials concluded that talks were going nowhere, they prepared for the use of force. They chose a time likely to attract the least resistance, and an aggressive intervention team designed to quickly subdue any residual resistance. In a predawn raid of the González home, federal agents burst through the crowd who were there to protect against such an action and subsequently smashed open the front door of the house with battering rams. Agents proceeded to the bedroom, where Elián was huddled with one of the men who rescued him the previous Thanksgiving. With military-style weapons raised, they demanded the child.

In the wake of the raid, the streets of Little Havana erupted in a riot. One report described the scene as "a gauntlet of concrete benches, garbage dumpsters, newspaper boxes, stop signs, chairs, and other objects thrown into the wide streets and burned" (*Time* 2000e). Again the conduct of dissent presented a question of meaning. For many, the riot confirmed a view of a petulant community. In the face of the bad publicity, some rationalized the response by arguing it was an overaggressive state that ultimately caused the raid. One man remarked, for example, that

> we are peaceful people. We are not violent. Look at what they have turned us into (*Time* 2000e).

For him, this was a community normally up to the duties of citizenship and maintaining its proper boundaries of order only prompted to transgress them when placed under the extreme pressure of outside intervention.

With the raid, the state forcefully crossed the boundary that marked off the public and the private in order to reassert its authority against dissenting citizens and local government officials. In the wake of the action, there was a flood of commentary, much of it focusing on an image that came to crystallize the relationship among citizens, the state, and space as played out in the saga of the boy from Cuba. The image—quickly circulated around the world to grace the following morning's front page—depicted a federal agent, in full paramilitary garb, pointing an automatic weapon at the head of Donato Dalrymple, one of the fishermen who had saved Elián from the ocean. The agent is demanding that Dalrymple hand over the child, who is seen shrieking in terror at the sight of the agent (see Figure 5.2).

But while much as the commentary focused on these four figures—the three protagonists and the gun—it also focused on *where* they were: the closet of the bedroom where the boy had been sleeping during the early-morning raid. For conservatives, this was a horrifying image of a tyrannical state that had overstepped the bounds of its authority and violated the sanctity of what conservative commentator Will described as a "peaceful American household" (*This Week* 2000). The failure of the state to respect the sanctity of the divide between the public space outside

Fig. 5.2 Emblematic media image of the raid of the González family home by federal agents. (Photograph courtesy of AP/Wide World Photos, used by permission.)

and the private realm within, Congressman Tom DeLay argued, blurred the moral line that distinguished the United States from other countries. The tyranny of this act, in other words, allowed an equivalence to be drawn to the tyrannical state of Cuba (*Meet the Press* 2000).

In interpreting the raid and the events preceding it, commentators argued by geopolitical analogy. Within an international perspective, the Right argued that the incident suggested the U.S. state was like Cuba. A *Miami Herald* editorial asked, "If the president believes the thug display by armed federal agents against a horrified 6-year-old child constitutes the right thing to do, then we must ask him this: What country do you govern, sir? Is it the United States or is it Cuba?" (*The Miami Herald* 2000g). In a survey of responses to the raid, one nursing student in Texas who otherwise supported the child's return to his father said,

> To me, it was something I would see if he were in Cuba. It just was not right, not in a family home, not in America. These people have done nothing, no aggression, no violence (*The Miami Herald* 2000h).

An exile in Miami replied similarly, "It's unforgivable what the government did. That's something you'd expect in communist Cuba or Hitler's Germany but not in the United States."

Within a national perspective, commentators often represented the conflict between the federal state and local dissidents by reference to the Civil Rights struggles of the 1960s. Critics of the administration compared the Miami Cuban community to the Civil Rights movement itself. "Pictures of the 6-year-old, screaming in terror, in the clutches of those who had put a gun in his face," Will argued, "demonstrate what leaders of America's Civil Rights movement understood: the power of graphic journalism when recording the brutal infliction of force to enforce injustice" (2000). Another editorial in *Newsweek* drew on a similar theme, saying, "In the 1960s, protesters at antiwar demonstrations chanted, 'Hell no, we won't go,' and were seen as brave resisters in the spirit of Mahatma Gandhi; today, protesters outside the Little Havana house holding signs reading 'Hell no, he won't go' have been seen for weeks by many critics as lawbreakers in the spirit of George Wallace" (Alter 2000).

Indeed, supporters of the raid and its reassertion of federal state authority over the lawless space of the González home also made comparisons with Civil Rights battles. Such rhetoric typically compared the Miami Cuban community with segregationists from the 1960s resisting the dismantling of the geographies of Jim Crow through the exercise of power exerted from elsewhere. One *Newsweek* article—quoting Miami-Dade County Mayor Alex Penelas' statement that "our local law-enforcement resources will not participate in the forced removal or repatriation of Elián González, which we would consider illegal"—likened it to "a Southern governor resisting school integration 40 years ago" (*Newsweek* 2000a).

National opinion polls had shown general support for returning the boy to his father. Public opinion was much more sharply divided on the raid, however. A bus driver in the Bronx explained his reaction this way: "This was like the cops saving him from kidnappers. After all the threats and the crazy ranting, it would have been crazy for them to go in without guns" (*The Miami Herald* 2000h).

Not surprisingly, interviews with supporters of the raid also focused on the image. Questions put to Deputy Attorney General Holder focused specifically on how the image would play on a global stage. And in an interesting recognition that symbolic violence is as much the preserve of the state as it is of those who would defy it, former Solicitor General Walter Dellinger explained in reference to the image that "a great show of force can often avoid violence" (*This Week* 2000). It is not just oppositional groups like the Zapatistas in Chiapas that make use of violence as theater, then, but in many cases the state itself.

Legacies

Among the vestiges of the conflict over Elián were two museums: one in Miami, and the other in the boy's Cuban hometown of Cardenas. The latter is typical socialist kitsch, reflected in everything from the building's name—*The Museum of the Battle of Ideas*—to the bronze statue of the boy upheld "by a sea of hands, representing the Cuban people" (*Washington Post* 2002). The museum in Miami is called Casa Elián or the Elián Museum and consisted of the preserved home that both sheltered the boy and which endured the violation of federal agents storming its doors.

During the course of the saga, Elián's image circulated over the airwaves and within concrete spaces. The Cuban government plastered Havana's crumbling facades with murals of the boy, and Cardenas was likewise awash in images. The image, however, also made its way elsewhere. In Moscow, a group holding signs of Elián protested outside the U.S. Embassy, demanding his return. And Elián's image also made its way to Seattle, to show up on posters lofted in the air amid the protests over the meetings of the WTO. What in the world did an international custody battle have to do with globalization and trade?

In some sense, absolutely nothing. The antiglobalization protests did, however, provide a stage on which activists of all stripes could dramatize their cause. "If the image of a child can be effective in campaigns like muscular dystrophy," a spokeswoman for the Cuban-American National Foundation explained, "then it can make people aware of Castro's victims" (*Time* 1999). For the Right, the child was a symbolic weapon that—because of the reservoirs of meaning associated with childhood itself—could be used to sharpen the moral lines that answer the question of where the boy ought to call home. Seattle provided a way to express broader discontents about various injustices in a context of otherwise radically different politics. In another respect, however, both the Elián González saga and the protest over economic globalization shared commonalities. They each centered on relationships between state power and citizenship, and the boundaries that define them.

6

Free Trade and Fences: Globalization and the Politics of Mobility in Québec City, 2001

In April 2001, as representatives from 34 states gathered in a conference center in Québec City for the annual meeting of the Summit of the Americas, activists from similarly diverse places gathered on the streets of the city. Summit delegates were in Québec City to discuss details of the proposed Free Trade Area of the Americas (FTAA), which would extend NAFTA over the space of the entire hemisphere (save for Cuba). Before leaving for the Summit, newly elected President George W. Bush noted that when implemented, the FTAA would create "the largest free trade area in the world, encompassing 34 countries and 800 million people" (Edwords 2001). More prosaically, Bush sounded a theme that would subsequently become much more prominent. "Our goal in Québec," he said, "is to build a hemisphere of liberty" (Edwords 2001).

Efforts such as the FTAA are often characterized as building blocks of a transparent and inevitable process of "globalization." Such a rendering portrays globalization as an almost-natural process and any resistance to it as futile. It would be more accurate, however, to characterize dominant rhetorics of globalization as embodying a rather more particular vision: one based on principles of neoliberalism. From this perspective, the future is envisioned normatively as one of fast-paced mobility. Goods and services could move across international borders with minimal resistance, providing consumers the freedom to choose among an unprecedented cornucopia of alternatives. Likewise, the world of neoliberal globalization is one of fluidly mobile capital, where corporations can easily move investments and productive facilities around the world. When George W. Bush spoke of creating a "hemisphere of liberty," then, he was imagining a borderless, free-flowing world that linked producer and consumer across arbitrary distances. Geography, in essence, no longer mattered.

The FTAA was thus yet another example of the boundary-eroding drive of economic globalization under neoliberal orthodoxy. Nevertheless, the supreme irony is that in the early 21st century, a summit dedicated to realizing neoliberal visions of liberty could only take place alongside significant efforts to limit it. Likewise, in a normative world of borderless mobility, boundaries were absolutely essential to the staging of the event. In the months before the Summit, Québec City, through unprecedented transformations in the urban security landscape, became a barricade city (Figure 6.1). Security officials erected a massive fence that wound 3.8 kilometers (2.4 miles) around the historic city center, bounding a 10-square-kilometer zone around the Summit site that barred any public access, never mind demonstrations. A pass system granted access across the boundary of the Fence only to designated residents, employees, accredited delegates, reporters, and others explicitly approved by authorities.

Canadian officials' efforts to secure order in Québec City were not limited to the space of the city, however. At the larger scale of state boundaries, Canadian authorities carefully regulated movement across the international border with an eye toward influencing

Fig. 6.1 Tearing down the walls of regulation. (Image courtesy of Artizans, used by permission.)

movement into Québec City. The focus of these efforts was to keep many activists away from Québec City altogether. Not unlike efforts by the FBI to limit the mobility of supporters of the Wounded Knee occupation in 1973, the Canadian state's efforts to constrain the mobility of certain people was likewise an attempt to shape the contours of dissent in public space. A politics of public space was thus inseparably a politics of scale.

The radical geosecurity engineering involved in staging the Summit of the Americas in Québec City raised deep questions not just about the nature of neoliberal globalization and its rather stunted rhetorics of freedom and liberty, but also about democratic citizenship itself in an era of globalization. Who should have what kind of rights to dissent in what kinds of ways? Equally important, *where* should they be allowed to express their dissent? Conversely, what length ought a liberal state go to ensure order, and at the expense of what liberties?

Seattle and the Antiglobalization Movement

The Summit of the Americas took place before the backdrop of more than a year of massive antiglobalization protests inaugurated in Seattle in late 1999 (Figure 6.1). Like Québec City, Seattle played host to a large international meeting dedicated to realizing neoliberal dreams of a hypermobile world unfettered by states or the collective rights and responsibilities their borders might contain. Delegates from over 130 countries went to Seattle to attend meetings of the World Trade Organization (WTO), whose purpose is to promote a world of freely mobile trade. As the organization itself rather innocently puts it, "The WTO is a place where member governments go, to try to sort out the trade problems they face with each other" (World Trade Organization 2005).

Up until 30 November 1999, the notion that a meeting to discuss the arcane rules and regulations associated with an international trade organization could attract tens of thousands of protesters was largely unthinkable to the American public. Yet by the end of the day, tens of thousands of protesters converged on the city. Trade unionists and environmentalists, anarchists and feminists, immigrants rights activists and indigenous people from far beyond Seattle all converged on the city's streets to energetically protest the WTO and all it was taken to represent. The organization presented an institutional face to the vast abstractions of neoliberal globalization.

Activists successfully shut down the meetings through aggressive tactics of confrontation. Their tactics consisted largely of strategically limiting the mobility of delegates within the city: denying their access to the site of the meetings. In response, the Seattle City Council issued a series of emergency orders designed to reassert control of the city's public spaces. Among them was the designation of a 25-block "no protest zone" that removed the right of assembly from the downtown spaces that hosted the meetings. In turn, police aggressively enforced the emergency orders. Images of smashed store windows and bloodied protesters dominated evening news broadcasts. The images alternately represented the heavy-handed weight of repressive state authority and the mindless violence of an anarchist fringe.

The intensely mediated spectacle of it all—coupled with activists' successful shutting down of the meetings—turned Seattle from an anonymous location in the business of free trade into a contested site in the larger contest over the future contours of global citizenship. If Chicago 1968 represented a larger conflict over the meaning of the United States and its relationship with the rest of the world, so too did Seattle 1999. Out of Seattle, the antiglobalization movement became part of a broader public discourse, and a significant political force.

Protesting Globalization

The very term "antiglobalization movement" is controversial and suggests a somewhat artificial coherence. "Antiglobalization is not one thing," Tom O'Connor argues, "but a complicated alliance of many different sectors including progressive trade unions, new social movements, and oppositional youth cultures" (2003). Nevertheless, in the wake of Seattle, this quite diverse and eclectic mix of groups and movements was now lumped together—some would argue largely by the media—under the banner of a larger umbrella called "antiglobalization," and there was broad—if often grudging—recognition across the political spectrum that this was a politically significant movement. The antiglobalization movement enjoyed momentum. It was organized across relatively extensive geographies, successful in making its presence felt at various subsequent international meetings focused on the business of neoliberal globalization, and politically visible.

The Summit of the Americas took place against this backdrop. Host to 34 heads of state and roughly 9,000 participants, it was the largest and most significant such meeting in Canadian history. Largely for this reason, the Summit was also host to tens of thousands of protesters. As they did in Seattle, and subsequently in Prague, Washington, Melbourne, and Davos, the activists were in Québec City to protest against the broader neoliberal project to rework the boundaries that mediate their lives. As with Seattle, for the protesters, the issues at stake with the FTAA were not narrowly about free trade. They also encompassed issues such as nature and immigrants' rights, patriarchy and xenophobia, indigenous rights and militarism.

The broad point was that the effort to cast questions of trade as exclusively about trade served precisely to obscure their more wide-ranging connections and contradictions. To privilege the mobility of capital was thus to disparage the mobility of labor and with that to contribute to a sometimes xenophobic anti-immigrant racism. To the degree that the project of neoliberal globalization worked to dissolve the boundaries to the free movement of goods and investment, it also served to dissolve the boundaries of collective rights and citizenship and to leave intact still other boundaries.

For the activists, the boundary politics of neoliberal globalization served to enable the freedom and mobility—and indeed power—of those individuals and organizations that were already the most privileged members of the global citizenry. Free trade simply presented multinational corporations greater freedom to take advantage of opportunities offered by various localities as they competed in a global competitive field. Likewise, the enhanced mobility offered by a globalizing economy also offered companies the freedom to avoid the unionized wage rates and regulations of developed economies and to exploit the low wages and relatively lax regulations of many developing economies (Brecher and Costello 1998). The enhanced capital mobility of neoliberal globalization created competitive pressures that drove down wages and labor conditions. For activists, the project of globalization was less about dissolving boundaries for the greater good of all—as Bush's rhetoric of a "hemisphere of liberty" would suggest—but rather in reconfiguring various boundaries in ways that selectively privileged an already global elite.

Although there were clearly issues at play in Québec City that had a somewhat different resonance than those dramatized south of the border—privatization was of particular concern, for example, as activists worried about its impact on Canada's vaunted social welfare state—these discourses on the contemporary geography of citizenship and marginality under globalization are broadly applicable to the constellation of movements associated with antiglobalization. In this sense, the articulation of dissent on the streets of Seattle and Québec City were quite similar in form and content.

Globalizing Protest

Although the events in Seattle and Québec City reflected significant protest *against* globalization, however, they also illustrated a more concrete transformation in the nature of protest itself. As much as they constituted a significant protest *of* globalization, the protests also illustrated the globalization of protest as well.

The transformation in the nature of protest as reflected in the antiglobalization movement was enabled in part by the very technologies that facilitated the complicated economic geographies of global multinational capital. Technologies such as the Internet, cell phones, and text messengers allowed for relatively efficient distributed organizing and information sharing, across large geographic distances. Satellite-connected television dramatically enhanced the technological ability to widely circulate images of the sort performed in the context of protest events. All of these technologies were central to the success of the antiglobalization movement. They made it easier to bring together a diversity of people with broadly similar interests in one space and to use that presence in space to widely circulate a particular political message.

Characterizing the new spatial relationships brought together in the antiglobalization movement's practices, Paul Routledge (2000, 2003) suggests the concept of "convergence space." Rather than conceive of a monolithic movement with unitary interests and politics, convergence space suggests instead a more complex and differentiated mingling of identities, politics, and interests. As he puts it:

> A convergence space implies a heterogeneous affinity of common ground between various social movements, grassroots initiatives, nongovernmental organizations, and other formations, wherein certain interests, goals, tactics, and strategies converge. It is a space of facilitation, solidarity, communication, coordination, and information sharing. It is both virtual—enacted through the Internet—and material, enacted through conferences and

various kinds of direct action such as demonstrations and strikes (2000: 25).

The concept also suggests a more complex view of the spatialities of such movements. If the antiglobalization movement is not one movement, but many—each of which is itself characterized by complex and dynamic interactions with spaces from the micro-level of the street and the city, to the larger spaces of national governments and global media—then the convergence space itself is all the more complex.

From this perspective, the antiglobalization movement is itself a product of globalization, if a more complex, contentious, and messy process than globalization as seen through the lens of trade delegates. Yet as much as the events in Seattle and Québec City reflected something new about the contemporary politics of global change and the technology of dissent, however, they also showed clear continuities with the politics of dissent in previous decades. Again, divisive political moments played out in city public spaces, as dissenters actively claimed those spaces and police aggressively sought to deny them such claims. Again, dissenters and police relied on geographical tactics in seeking to effect their will on city public spaces. Activists relied on creative communications strategies to coordinate their convergence on Seattle, as well as novel street theater to dramatize their claims and make them media-friendly. Again dissent in public space became mediated spectacle, the meaning and impact of the event as much about the virtual spaces of television and the newspaper as about the streets of Seattle.

Since 1999, a variety of other sites where large institutions with global reach and influence meet have also become sites of massive protests. Prague, Melbourne, Bangkok, Washington, and New York—to name but a few—have been wracked by protests against institutions taken to represent an ominous force called globalization: the IMF, the World Bank, the WTO. Protesters have not just creatively dramatized the symbolic politics of globalization, but have also creatively used its instruments—most notably cell phones and the Internet—to organize. The frequency and intensity of the protests have prompted states to adopt similarly novel tactics to maintain order and contain dissent. The remainder of this chapter thus analyzes these dynamics in the context of one particular protest event: that which took place in Québec City in April of 2001.

Boundaries and the Politics of Mobility in Québec City

Mobility Rights and Public Space in a Barricaded City

The large issues about the boundaries that contain—or not, as it were—states and economies, identity and power, rights and responsibilities also played out over a variety of other kinds of boundaries. In the months before the Summit, Québec City was transformed into a "barricaded city." Security officials and planners radically transformed both the physical landscape around the Summit site, as well as the very content of its public spaces. The city's most significant public spaces were—for a period of time—transformed into something else entirely. The officials charged with ensuring order in Québec City's streets argued such measures were necessary to avoid the kind of anarchy seen in Seattle. As Québec Minister for Public Security Serge Menard put the matter rather menacingly months before the event, "If you want peace, you must prepare for war" (Leroux 2001a).

The Summit took place before the backdrop of more than a year of major civil unrest that accompanied meetings of the WTO in Seattle, the IMF in Washington, and the World Bank in Prague. With that hindsight [15], the security arrangements around the Summit were the most elaborate in Canadian history. A committee coordinated security among the Royal Canadian Mounted Police (RCMP), the armed forces, the Québec City Police Department, and the Sainte-Foy Department of Public Safety (*Tremblay v. Québec* [Attorney General] 2001). They involved over 6,000 security personnel, drawn from across Canada. The RCMP, according to one report, sealed all sewer entrances in the area around the Summit location, "rented all the vacant apartments and houses within the security perimeter, and reserved all the hotel rooms—to keep troublemakers out" (Leroux 2001b). Québec security officials also emptied a local prison during the event to provide space for arrestees.

The primary spatial technology officials used to ensure order in the city was the Fence. The 2-meter-high chain link fence stood on large concrete blocks and wound 3.8 kilometers through the historic city center, encircling a 10-square-kilometer space. Eight high-security checkpoints filtered access into and out of the space bound by the Fence. Two further mechanisms regulated movement across that boundary. The first was a pass system that granted access to those roughly 25,000 people with legitimate long-term claims to that space based on either work or residence. The other was an accreditation system that certified people with more transitory—but still officially legitimate— reasons to be in the city center during the course of the meetings: some 5,000 delegates and roughly 3,000 media personnel (Leroux 2001a).

The Fence thus barred access to the city center to everyone else (and the majority of Québec City residents, in fact). Moreover, those who did manage access beyond the Fence could not partic- ipate in legal demonstrations, as the city police department had an explicit policy to deny permits. In addition, they found them- selves subject to an obscure local ordinance that banned wearing clothing that might obscure one's face, such as bandannas. The purpose of the measure, no doubt, was to ensure better visibility of occupants of public space and to target particular individual troublemakers. Together, these measures reflected an aggressive effort to ensure order in a post-Seattle context.

The aggressive security measures brought predictable reaction from civil rights activists. One Vancouver-based lawyer and activ- ist put the issue in stark terms when she argued that the measures constituted a "criminalization of dissent" that had effectively "established apartheid" (Grace 2001). She drew the connection between South Africa and Québec by virtue of the fact that, in both cases, state power was exercised through the regulation of bodily mobility. As she put it, "you need passes to move in and out." The label that critics attached to the Fence—the "Wall of Shame"—was itself meant to suggest two other boundaries: the

Berlin Wall and the Wall of Shame and Death dividing El Paso and Ciudad Juarez. One activist explained the symbolism like so:

> The Berlin Wall ... separated ideology and territory in the service of statist imperialism and the Wall of Shame and Death ... separating the Americas, not on the basis of ideology, but on the basis of economic exploitation; dividing the haves from the have-nots; the mythical El Dorado of the North from the barrios of the South; the illusory kingdom of capital from the regions where wealth originates and poverty reigns (Bobiwash 2003).

For critics, the Fence represented a fundamentally undemocratic privatization of public space; part of a broader bundle of tactics that collectively served to shrink the boundaries of permissible dissent by regulating who could move where, and in so doing shape the content—and the practice—of public space itself.

Yet it was not only activists and lawyers who were uneasy about the citizenship implications of the Summit security measures. One self-described "free-trader," for example, wrote of his experience observing firsthand the aggressive policing tactics used during the Summit:

> Yes, the delegates' security must be guaranteed, and the violent elements must be controlled. But at what cost? And when police attack peaceful protesters, who is to blame when more violence results (McElravy 2001)?

This free-trade proponent was concerned about the political contradictions of on one hand promoting a rhetoric of liberty, while on the other heavily circumscribing it.

Others were concerned about the negative economic impact. One local restaurant owner, for example, commented:

> You think of the images of Québec being transmitted around the planet, the publicity, the contacts for the future, all the extra business for hotels, boutiques, restaurants. ... We don't have much information so far, but everything in

the news seems to be negative. … [N]ow there's all this talk of having local residents wear identity cards and barricading whole sectors of the city for anyone who doesn't have accreditation. Sure, you need security, but couldn't that provoke them even more (*The Toronto Star* 2000)?

For this business owner, the contradictions of the Fence extended beyond symbolism to the very heart of the economic matter. In aggressively working to maintain order, he suggested, officials were limiting the very thing they sought to promote: a world of freely mobile goods and consumers.

The erection of the Fence also reflected the more general tension within liberal democracy between the right to freely dissent and the need for order. A spokesperson for a Québec legal rights organization put the tension—and the need to strike a reasonable balance—like so:

The necessity to establish a security perimeter shouldn't transform the provincial capital into a city under siege, where the fundamental rights of civil society to express itself cannot be exercised in public space (Leroux 2001b).

The Fence thus represented an ambivalent spatial moment in Canada's historical geography of citizenship and symbolized the inherent contradictions of liberal democracy.

This tension—between the need for order and the freedom to dissent—was the subject of a legal suit brought before the Québec Provincial Court by Montréal-based attorney Marc Tremblay. On 29 January 2001, Tremblay contacted the Québec City Police Department to ask for a pass to enter the space beyond the Fence during the Summit. As he wrote in an application letter:

I wish to conduct an individual and peaceful demonstration. My demonstration is not intended to disrupt the Summit in any way, nor is it intended to prevent anyone from entering the Convention Centre or any other place, nor to breach the peace, nor to disrupt the movements of the dignitaries or other persons attending the Summit of the Americas (*Tremblay v. Québec* [Attorney General] 2001).

Despite being told no such passes would be granted for the purposes of demonstrations, Tremblay persisted in formally applying for the pass. The application was rejected.

Tremblay then sought judicial relief. He claimed that the Fence—and officials' refusal to allow him to cross it—violated a variety of his fundamental rights under the Canadian Charter. They violated his ability to freely express himself, his right to be presumed innocent until proven guilty, and his freedom to assemble in spaces and at times of his own choosing. In addition, all of this was tied together around mobility rights: the ability to move from place to place.

Central to Tremblay's constitutional argument was his assertion that in using the Fence to limit his right to move, security officials also limited his ability to freely assemble in space and to speak. Tremblay couched his rights claims in narrowly drawn, individualistic terms. He presented his case in the most non-threatening of ways: as an individual. He wanted access to the meeting site in order conduct a peaceful demonstration of one. He explicitly noted his aims were purely communicative; that he had no intention of disrupting the meetings in any way, other than through the power of persuasive speech.

And yet, he argued, embodied speech—rather than simply mediated images—needed to be geographically present to be heard by the proper audience and to be persuasive. Tremblay's argument rooted his critique of the Fence on central tenets of liberal rights, cast with an explicitly spatial orientation. The Fence, he argued, limited the capacity to speak freely because it limited the freedom to assemble in space and to move across it. Speech untethered to geography, he recognized, is not truly free. There is a gap, in other words, between the right to move and the right to assemble. The ability to move in general does not necessarily mean the ability to move to any location in particular, and location—as geographers are wont to emphasize—is often everything.

The relief Tremblay sought was rather more broad than the narrowly drawn claims he was making, however. He asked the court to halt construction of the Fence and to direct authorities to allow demonstrations. If the Fence violated Tremblay's individual rights to move within the city and to assemble in public space to express dissent, he requested the court intervene to protect the interests of all Canadian citizens by completely removing *any* impediments to either assembly or mobility within the city. Absent this, Tremblay requested he be issued an individual pass to move freely within the space bounded by the Fence. A supporting attorney proposed further alternatives to the court, all of which involved freeing up the capacity to move within the city center and to conduct peaceful demonstrations.

The Fence, of course, was aimed precisely at regulating who could move where in the city. It established a selectively permeable boundary around the city center. The space bounded by the Fence contained the city's most important public spaces. Those very same spaces were to be the venue for a meeting that presented unique security challenges. As the court interpreted the fundamental spatial contradiction:

> The streets, sidewalks, and squares of the Upper Town of Québec City are public places, where all citizens should be able to express themselves using all the means at their disposal as long as they do not contravene legal or regulatory provisions. However, for three days from this Friday, 20 April, the political authorities have chosen this public space rather than government property as the venue for an international relations exercise. Unprecedented in terms of its scale in Canada, this economic summit will host 34 heads of state from throughout the Americas in the centre of Québec City (*Tremblay v. Québec* [Attorney General] 2001: Paragraph 60).

For authorities, this presented an unresolvable problem: One space could simply not contain such disparate interests, practices, and bodies. Their solution was thus to privatize the city's central public spaces for the 3 days of the meetings and displace anti-FTAA gatherings elsewhere.

Officials took pains to argue that the FTAA meetings were somewhat unique in the context of international meetings relating to neoliberal free trade. They were to bring together an almost unprecedented group of heads of state. Given the history of major civil unrest associated with such meetings, and the stated intention of some groups to go to the Summit, officials argued, the aggressive security measures—including the Fence—were more than justified. Security officials wished to completely banish any potential disorder from the city center. Instead, they planned to move the spaces of dissent elsewhere. Planners arranged for demonstration sites in other locations in the city, including three in close proximity to the Fence. Still, this raised the question of whether such relatively marginal protest sites were equivalent to being at the site of the meetings themselves. The court put the matter like so:

> Aside from the major disruptions to local residents, the security fence keeps citizens who merely wish to attend the event or demonstrate peacefully far away from the heart of matters. Specifically in the case of protesters, the fence makes it impossible to enter into any direct visual or audio communication with the people whom they wish to address, namely the heads of state of the 34 countries taking part in talks to set up the FTAA (*Tremblay v. Québec* [Attorney General] 2001: Paragraph 82).

The spatial conflict, then, was not simply about *whether* public dissent would be permitted in Québec City, but *where*.

The legal question revolved around whether such regulation—and the inherent limitations on the rights of some—was balanced against the need to ensure order for others. In assessing the case, the court was required to weigh the abstract legal claim, as well as the concrete contextual issues that might intervene in determining the reasonableness of the security measures. The court agreed with Tremblay that the Fence limited certain fundamental liberties under the Charter. Specifically, it wrote that "the freedom of expression and of peaceful assembly has definitely been limited" (*Tremblay v. Québec* [Attorney General] 2001: Paragraph 63).

The issue before the court, however, was not just whether the Fence violated particular rights of individuals, but whether such violations were reasonable. The court concluded they were indeed:

> The recent experiences of Prague and Seattle, among others, demonstrate clearly that in the current context of protests over globalisation, it is sadly necessary when organising a major economic summit to erect a security fence to seal off the area in which delegates are to move around. The aim is to avoid, as far as possible, any potentially violent confrontation between the forces of order and a large mass of protesters including rioters who are impossible to identify and control (*Tremblay v. Québec* [Attorney General] 2001: Paragraph 77).

This argument drew on two prominent themes. First, context matters in assessing rights. That context included, on one hand, an aggressive antiglobalization movement with a history of violent confrontation, and on the other hand an event of major scope and importance that would attract significant attention from these same groups. The second theme—expressed a number of places in the ruling—was less matter-of-fact and more evocative of the larger stakes involved: that in the face of faceless rioters "impossible to identify and control," the "forces of order" must adopt novel tactics in response. The Fence was just such a novel tactic.

Likewise, the court rejected out of hand Tremblay's claim that the Fence violated his right to be presumed innocent. Tremblay argued that the very fact of a pass system presumed an entire class of people—indeed, the majority of Québec City citizens—to be potential troublemakers and lawbreakers, and thus that they were by default presumed guilty. The court disagreed, noting there was no explicit charge against Tremblay and thus that he had not been formally presumed guilty.

Perhaps most interestingly, the court rejected what was arguably Tremblay's central claim: that the Fence violated his mobility rights. Liberal constructions of mobility tend both to privilege individual mobility against collective and to be drawn more tightly around residence and work than the transitory movement of bodies across space. Article 6 of the Canadian Charter, for example, states that citizens and permanent residents have the right "to move to and take up residence in any province," and "to pursue the gaining of livelihood in any province." As the court noted in assessing Tremblay's claims, this is a decidedly more limited notion of mobility than the expansive one held by the plaintiff.

The court's reading of mobility rights was consistent with Canadian precedent. Blomley (1994) has noted that Canadian courts have tended to construct mobility rights in ways that privilege individual rights. They have given fairly broad protection, for example, to movement in search of economic opportunities, or to be free from sanctions that penalize such movement. On the other hand, the courts have tended to be much more deeply suspicious of collective rights. The case study he presents is of a mill town in British Colombia devastated by a company's decision to close its factory there and move it to Mexico. The issue here was the right of a company—seen in the eyes of law as an individual—to freely move, measured against whatever duties of corporate citizenship it owed to the town as a collectivity. In both this case and in *Tremblay v. Québec*, courts rejected readings of mobility that cast it in expansive terms. The right to mobility, they argued, was not absolute; it applied for the most part to individuals and was less the sort of short-term mobility on which political activism is based than that of the longer-term freedom of a citizen—constructed in narrowly legal and economic terms—to move residence.

Boundaries of Sovereignty

> BOUNDARY, n. In political geography, an imaginary line
> between two nations, separating the imaginary rights of
> one from the imaginary rights of the other.

— Ambrose Bierce, *The Devil's Dictionary*

Clearly much of the conflict over the FTAA was played out on the
stage of Québec City and its public spaces. And it was resolved in
those concrete spaces more than in the reserved space of the
courtroom and the abstractions of law. Although the court
rejected Tremblay's suit and the Fence remained, activists claimed
the city's public spaces nonetheless. People wove ribbons through
the Fence, transforming it into a space symbolic of something
other than what it appeared at face value. Later, a group of activists managed to tear down portions of the Fence. Although not
successful in shutting down the Summit as the activists in Seattle
had been, they successfully registered their dissent through the
medium of public space.

Yet the geographic dynamics of the protests in Québec City
extended far beyond the city and the boundary that contained it.
During the meeting, another important issue both for the Canadian state and for activists was who would be allowed to cross the
border. One of those activists interested in moving across the
border and on to Québec City was then-85-year-old David Dellinger. Dellinger had an entire lifetime of activism behind him.
During World War II, he went to jail over his refusal to submit to
conscription. In the 1960s, he was a major figure in the movement against the Vietnam War. He was perhaps most famous for
his role in organizing the protests that took place at Chicago in
1968 and was one of the Chicago Eight initially prosecuted under
the *H. Rap Brown Act*. In 1973, he expressed his solidarity with
Wounded Knee occupiers by traveling to the site, in the process
likely violating the very law he had previously been prosecuted
under. Dellinger, put simply, was for many security officials precisely the sort of "outside agitator" that gave them pause, even if
he was a rather elderly one (1975).

As in Chicago in 1968, the Summit of the Americas was the occasion for another important protest event for Dellinger. As he put it optimistically, "I think that for the first time that we have an actual ability to change the system" (Smith 2001). Despite his activist background, Dellinger was allowed—most likely because of his age—to cross the border and move on to Québec. Yet although the famous activist was allowed to travel to Québec City, many others were turned away, particularly those with arrest records or, as a CBS News report (Smith 2001) put it, those with "an attitude." If in Québec City officials constructed a new boundary to filter access into the city center by selectively limiting the mobility of some, in this case border officials made use of an existing international geopolitical boundary to achieve the same effect. In each, the goal was the same: to regulate who could move where vis-à-vis the site of the Summit of the Americas.

Anticipating just this mobility problem, rumors spread on the Internet among activist circles that the Akwesasne Mohawk Nation had offered its territory as a corridor that would allow activists to circumvent Canadian customs. As one Indian nation whose territory is bisected by the international border that divides the United States and Canada, some Akwesasne activists offered protesters access across the border (*Montreal Gazette* 2001). Despite the trumpeting of the New World Order that accompanies the dissolving boundaries of the contemporary world—and beyond the boundary-erasing impetus behind the FTAA—for Native America boundaries have been of long-standing importance. The six nations that make up the Iroquois Confederacy—known simply as the Six Nations—have a particularly strong history of asserting their sovereignty. In recent years, the international border has figured prominently. In 1997, for example, Grand Chief Mike Mitchell of the Akwesasne Mohawks filed suit against the Canadian government over its authority to levy customs duties against members of the tribe (*Mitchell v. Canada* 1997). Mitchell argued that both the territorial recognition written in treaties and the historical geography of ancestral trading territories established Mohawk sovereignty rights that trumped those of the Canadian state itself. Indeed, in assessing the sovereignty claims of the Akwesasne vis-à-vis the international border, the judge noted, "What is at issue in the present case ... is what constituted Mohawk territory."

The judge supported the plaintiff's sovereignty claims and their implicit arguments in support of mobility rights unrestricted by an artificially imposed border. The argument was firmly historical and geographical:

> With respect to the use of the territory in and around Akwesasne for the purposes of trade, I am satisfied that the Mohawks traveled across the boundary from their homeland in the United States into Canadian territory for trade-related purposes prior to the arrival of the Europeans. The Mohawks crossed the boundary with their goods for personal and community use without having to pay duty or taxes on those goods. Whatever goods they obtained either by raiding or by hunting and fishing could be freely brought back across the border (*Mitchell v. Canada* 1997).

The legal judgment that came out of this historical geographic interpretation recognized a partial sovereignty for the Mohawk. "I find," the judge wrote, "that the plaintiff and the Mohawks of Akwesasne have established an aboriginal right to pass and repass freely what is now the Canada–United States boundary with goods for personal and community use and for trade with other First Nations."

In 2001, the border and the competing sovereignties that it dramatized was at issue again. A common theme for Akwesasne activists was the everyday indignity of being forced to submit to the authority of Canadian and American border officials. One activist—Shawn Brant—argued that "[t]he border is a barrier to community life in Akwesasne." He went on to say that "[i]t is the right of the Mohawk Nation to determine who can cross the border" (Zwarenstein 2001). Another Mohawk activist, John Boots, explained the everyday geopolitics of mobility around the border. "Sometimes it takes hours just to go get my mail 3 miles away,"

Boots explained. In part because of his status as an activist, he continued, "I get pulled over on the way there and pulled over on the way back."

The Summit of the Americas—and the manner in which Canadian officials were planning to use the border to regulate movement into Québec—provided an opportunity for Akwesasne activists to dramatize alternative understandings of territorial sovereignty, mobility, and boundaries. Brant, for example, saw it as an opportunity both to dramatize Mohawk sovereignty during the Summit and also to prepare for future efforts to reassert such territorial authority, all by reasserting control over mobility:

> My motivation is to assert and reinforce the sovereign integrity of Mohawk people within the Mohawk Nation and to bring the organizing bodies together so we can stand and fight in preparation for the fall. ... We will engage in attacks against the provincial economy, the provincial infrastructure. We will shut down highways, roadways, bridges until this government is brought to its knees (Zwarenstein 2001).

Like Tremblay in his lawsuit against the Fence that ringed the Québec City historic center, these activists sought to dramatize the enduring presence of boundaries and the less-than-fully-democratic authority they gave shape to.

The activists also saw their efforts as contributing to a broader solidarity effort: that if the FTAA could contribute to highlighting issues of indigenous sovereignty, so too could issues of native sovereignty be used to dramatize the concerns at issue with the free trade treaty. As Boots further explained the larger issues involved,

> The reason why we're helping them is we align ourselves with their protests as the poor people of Canada, the U.S., and Mexico . ... It's amazing how many of our aspirations are parallel (Hanes 2001).

As much as they sought to highlight the boundaries that continued to divide, they did so to recognize commonalities across borders.

To affirm this perspective, activists throughout North American border regions conducted cross-border solidarity actions. The Stop the FTAA coalition organized a cross-border protest at the United States–Mexico border at Tijuana–San Diego, while other regional groups did the same at United States–Canada border locations in both Washington and in the Northeast. The New York City-based Ya Basta! Collective planned to dramatize alternative notions of citizenship and boundaries with an action at the crossing at Champlain, NY, that included distributing world passports (Leroux 2001c).

Antiglobalization and Boundaries of Citizenship

> We expected this. You can't have a trade summit these days without tear gas; it would be like having a cheeseburger without the cheese.
>
> — Senior Bush administration official
> (*Newsweek* 2001)

The Akwesasne community was hardly unified in its support of openly defying the authority of the Canadian state. Indeed, the tactics by which these activists sought to highlight the conflict over Akwesasne sovereignty was a divisive one. Grand Chief Mitchell, for example, was against the action, worrying about the repercussions. As he put it:

> It is fair to say people are not in favour of this. ... They don't like this negative image and they are resentful that when people try to use the border to their own gain it always seems to be in connection with Akwesasne and that portrays us as a lawless society (Hanes 2001).

During a community meeting to discuss the issue, Mitchell showed a video of the unrest in Seattle, as if to emphasize the potential for anarchy that might accompany any action that supported the antiglobalization movement.

As with the unrest of the 1960s, the antiglobalization protests that erupted in Seattle and Québec City presented a crisis of interpretation and of citizenship. To the degree one can generalize about the antiglobalization movement, one can say that in part it offers an alternative language of citizenship rights to either the cosmopolitan individualism of neoliberalism or the more collective nationalism associated with a Keynesian era. That alternative is not entirely coherent, but in general might be characterized as a cosmopolitan vision of social justice. The language of rights is in general collective, but one that recognizes commonalities that span national borders. It thus presents challenges in locating—and indeed bounding—citizenship and sovereignty.

As in Chicago 1968 and Seattle 1999, one interpretation saw in the violence an overaggressive state maintaining its own authority and legitimacy at the expense of basic liberal rights. In the weeks after the Summit, Amnesty International issued a press release calling for a formal investigation into the state's aggressive policing of the Summit. The group cited excessive use of tear gas, unnecessary use of plastic bullets and electro-shock devices, and the sequestering of arrestees in cramped conditions away from legal representation (Amnesty International 2001).

Critics focused instead on the violence of the protestors and their politics. They were often similar to interpretations of Seattle, exemplified by an editorial published in *Time* shortly after the WTO protests. Titled "*Return of the Luddites*," it argued:

> The left professes concern for Third World labor. But its real objective is to keep jobs at home. That means stopping the jobs from going to the very campesinos it claims to champion—and sentencing Third World workers to the deprivation of the preindustrial life they so desperately seek to escape (Krauthammer 1999).

For critics like this, the globalization of protest evidenced in Seattle simply allowed the intensely local interests and political perspectives of the protesters to be made into a global spectacle that masked their lack of real political substance.

Among the more cynical interpretations of the antiglobalization movement in mainstream media circles were those of Fareed Zakaria. Zakaria interpreted Seattle as the resurgence of a worldview that he thought was no longer appropriate in a contemporary world of neoliberal globalization. Speaking in a language of cosmopolitan globalism and concern for the plight of the poor in the Global South, Zakaria argued, the antiglobalization movement masked a thoroughly antiquated and parochial perspective. As he put it:

> The idea that American workers will gain from slowing down, shutting off, or further regulating trade has no basis in history, economic theory, or common sense. It is simply a frightened reaction to change (1999).

This is by now a commonsense interpretation of the antiglobalization movement: that if it critiques neoliberal principles of free trade and free markets, it is antitrade and antimarkets, which reflects an irrational fear of change and a nostalgia for a distant past.

Roughly 18 months later, Zakaria again raised similar themes about the ultimate superficiality of the antiglobalization movement. His argument rested on three fundamental points. First, the kind of dissent performed in the streets of Seattle and Québec City was fundamentally deviant and thus illegitimate. "By taunting the police, beating drums, and throwing rocks," he wrote, "the rioters make it pretty clear that they want not a rational debate but the world's attention" (2001). For Zakaria, "beating drums" was not a legitimate part of the practice of citizenship; "rational debate," by contrast, was.

The second, closely connected, point was that the activists' tactics of dissent were deviant as well because they were out of place. The proper sphere of citizenship for Zakaria was a clearly liberal notion of a rational world of talk rooted in legislative chambers and ballot boxes. The activists, by contrast, relied on a mediated public sphere to circumvent their ultimate irrelevance to the real business of citizenship.

> It is trying to achieve, through intimidation and scare tactics, what it has not been able to get through legislation. The lesson of Seattle seems to be: If you cannot get your way through traditional democratic methods, through campaigns, lobbying, and legislatures, then riot and rabble-rouse on television. In the bizarre atmospherics of the modern media, when a few thousand trained protesters surround the elected presidents and prime ministers of 34 countries, the protesters gain the moral high ground (Zakaria 2001).

This rather Habermasian outlook renders the aggressive politics of dissent associated in the public imagination with the antiglobalization movement as fundamentally deviant both because of the nature of the tactics and because they have a disproportionate influence by virtue of the media. Again, we see the old themes of the insubstantiality of mediated protest and of how a deviant group of outsiders exploit the potentials it opens up.

Finally, Zakaria argued that the ultimate problem with the antiglobalization movement was that its antidemocratic character also manifest in a perversely anticosmopolitan globalism. The antiglobalization movement, Zakaria suggested, was not international enough. As he wrote,

> The leaders of antiglobalization now advocate policies for their own sheltered communities in rich Western countries. Of course, they claim their policies will help workers in Africa and Asia. But they won't. What developing countries need more than anything else—yes, even more than new labor and environmental regulations—is economic growth. And yet every proposal made by the protesters would slow down that growth and keep the Third World mired in medieval poverty. So much for international solidarity (2001).

From this perspective, the antiglobalization movement was a mass of contradictions. While speaking in the language of global justice, critics like Zakaria charged, their politics were profoundly local.

On CBS's *Face the Nation*, political pundit Bob Schieffer made broadly similar arguments, though focusing more on the issue of representation and politics. Schieffer seemed particularly troubled by the eclectic mix of seemingly disconnected issues dramatized during the protests. "A protest about everything," he argued, "is a protest about nothing, and that's a nuisance" (Schieffer 2001). The antiwar and women's rights protests of earlier decades worked, in a way he felt Québec City did not, because they were focused clearly on single issues. Instead, the antiglobalization movement, Schieffer asserted, had incoherent and internally contradictory politics that made its meaning illegible.

It is arguable whether the politics at issue on the streets of Seattle and Québec City were really as incoherent, or past examples as clear and focused, as Schieffer suggests. It may well be the case that the emerging language of the geography of citizenship—the spatial anchoring of rights and responsibilities—articulated in these (anti)globalizing protests is not as clear and coherent as it may yet be. But the underlying issues articulated by activists, despite their significant diversity, are quite clear.

Critics like Zakaria seemed troubled by the irony that the antiglobalization movement creatively used the very technologies of a mediated globalization to dramatize their concerns. For the critics, this allowed for the marginal perspectives of the protesters to gain much wider exposure and political reach than they would have otherwise. "What we saw in Seattle," Zakaria argued in the wake of Seattle,

> is the rise of a new kind of politics. Disparate groups, organized through the Internet and other easy means of communication, pursue at the supranational level what they cannot accomplish at the national level (Zakaria 1999).

The desire to declare the new is no less strong in critics of the antiglobalization movement than its champions. It is striking to note here, however, the strong parallels to arguments made more than 25 years before with respect to Wounded Knee and no doubt significantly farther back in time and in other sites. Indeed, the trope of the "outside agitator" exploiting the potentials of mediated public spheres by stirring up trouble in public space is an old one.

The irony is that critics like Zakaria ascribe a coherence to the "antiglobalization movement" that arguably is a product of the critics themselves, all to critique its internal contradictions. Such criticisms reflect both a certain level of cynicism, as well as a rather conventional understanding of the relationships between geographical boundaries and the politics of citizenship that may no longer be relevant to a globalized world. As another article, this one about Seattle, put it,

> Hitherto, it's been easy to insist that anyone opposed to "trade" was by definition a protectionist, happy to hide behind the walls of the nation-state. That simple equation no longer holds good; one of the most important lessons of Seattle is that there are two visions of globalization on offer, one led by commerce, one by social activism (Elliott 1999: 38).

Subsequent protests in Washington, Prague, Genoa, and Québec City (Drainville 2002) suggest that perhaps there is something more to the antiglobalization movement than critics profess.

At issue in the new social movements woven together under the banner of "antiglobalization" is both a new language of the geographies of citizenship and new approaches to the practice of dissent in public space. As Duncombe interprets the latter,

> In this new style of mass action there are no marches or speakers. Instead the goal is to occupy public space and transform it through blockades, lock downs, or, in the case of RTS affinity groups, clowning and dancing (2002: 228).

What unites many of these groups, he argues, is "shared distate for spectator-style politics" (Duncombe 2002: 228).

More broadly, the point of the protests in Québec City was precisely to throw into relief the *politics* of trade; to make it less an abstract process than a grounded practice. In surveying the controversy over the FTAA, no greater free-trade booster than *The Economist* noted that for all the talk of liberty at the center of the free-trade arguments of President Bush, in practice the United States had a quite ambivalent—often self-serving—position on trade (*The Economist* 2001). The Brazilian government's hesitancy over the FTAA, the magazine suggested, was not entirely irrational:

> Brazil's greatest fear is that the United States is plotting to stop it from becoming a big exporter of high-value manufactured goods and to make it return to its historic role of churning out low-value commodities. This is not entirely paranoia. The United States currently applies a whole range of duties, quotas, price restraints, and other measures to processed items from Brazil.

Despite the claim by critics that the antiglobalization of the North ultimately hurts the poor of the Global South, many of the most trenchant critiques of neoliberal globalization come from precisely there. Those critiques are often articulated in the streets. In the past decade, ordinary people in places otherwise worlds apart—from the streets of Bangkok (Glassman 2002) and Arequipa, Peru, to the jungles and small towns of Southern Mexico—have expressed remarkably consistent arguments against the direction of contemporary economic and political change under the pressures of neoliberal globalization. Those critiques often center on the gradual and selective erosion of the boundaries that contain the capacity for states to ensure the rights of citizenship.

7

Quarantining Dissent

If there is no place to freely assemble, there is no free assembly. If there is no place to freely express, there is no free expression.

— Reclaim the Streets

Wherever threatened, the first thing power restricts is the ability to linger or assemble in the street.

— Henri Lefebvre (2003 [1970]: 20)

Dissent and the broader politics of citizenship, I have argued, is a fundamentally geographical process. A variety of different kinds of spaces—delineated through a variety of different kinds of boundaries—provide media through which rights and identity are given form, contested, and redefined. As such, they can provide insight into larger practices of citizenship and state power.

Public space provides the most concrete of spatial media through which citizens materialize their dissent. It provides a theater of bodies in space, where identity and power is both displayed and contested. In each of the case studies I have presented, public space has provided both a material venue and a representational platform that dramatized the more specific issues at play. In debates about public unrest in 1968, public spaces provided media through which citizens expressed collective dissent: about the projection of American power abroad and the racial logics that disciplined urban spaces within. At the same time, such events provided occasions for larger debates about the rights and duties of citizenship. Likewise, in the more recent cases of antiglobalization protests and the conflict over Elián González, access to public space was central.

Communications media provide another important spatial medium that is wrapped up in the larger politics of citizenship and dissent. At Wounded Knee in 1973, activists seized the historic site and erected various boundaries to contain it as means to dramatize the broader boundary politics of American Indian sovereignty. They did this, however, primarily through their ability to turn that space into a platform through which to reach distant publics via the relatively new world of television news. Without activists' simultaneous material control of space and their savvy efforts to make it legible to a mediated public, the occupation would never have been the spectacle that it was; arguably it might not even have happened to begin with. Likewise with the Elián González case, which was simultaneously an intense expression of community identity in public spaces and an intensely mediated spectacle.

Rights to public space, however, are also formalized in the more abstract space of law. In all of the case studies, an important part of the geographical dynamics of the conflict was legal. Laws provide states bureaucratic instruments to regulate dissent that are simultaneously geographical. The *H. Rap Brown Act* emerged in 1968 as a product of the larger concern with what its sponsors regarded as the breakdown of state-sanctioned citizenship. Laying the problems of public unrest at the foot of "outside agitators," they sought to shrink the boundaries of permissible dissent by more tightly constraining the ability of activists to move across space and so to move between significant sites of protest and other spaces of public dissent. In turn, roughly 5 years later, the Nixon administration used this law to aggressively contain the lawless space of the Wounded Knee occupation. If the Wounded Knee occupiers sought to "jump scales" through media exposure and to sustain the occupation through tangible spatial connections, the state worked to actively circumscribe and to contain the site precisely to preclude that. In rather similar ways, the Canadian state also worked to manage the conduct of dissent in Québec City in 2001 by controlling the ability of activists to assemble in space through limiting their ability to move.

Finally, the geopolitics of law are simultaneously a geopolitics of mobility. The networks through which people and things move across space also provide important geographical contexts to the dynamics of dissent. Who is allowed to move, in what kinds of way, and with what effect were significant issues at stake in all of the case studies. The debates that raged in 1968 about "outside agitators" largely involved concern about the unchecked mobility of a certain class of people. Likewise, during both the occupation of Wounded Knee in 1973 and the protests in Québec City in 2001, different actors actively intervened either to constrain the capacity of certain people to move freely or, on the part of those same people, to evade such technologies of control. The debate about where Elián González should call home was also centered on the conditions under which people moved; in this case across international borders.

9/11: Geography, Dissent, and the "War on Terrorism"

As I write this early in 2005, it is difficult to contemplate the themes of this book—the intersections of citizenship, dissent, and the politics of boundaries—without considering the events of September 11, 2001, and the subsequent "War on Terror." The events of 9/11 were, if nothing else, a global spectacle. With simple yet bloody force, 19 hijackers turned the most innocuous instruments of globalization into deadly weapons, severely damaging the seat of American military power and leveling—with absolutely spectacular effect—a symbol of American capitalism. That the destruction of the World Trade Center towers had quite concrete effects on lives lost, on the landscape of a great city, and on the larger economy in which it sits is clear. Yet 9/11 was also a media event. Millions around the world saw the WTC fall to the ground in real-time. And, in public spaces around the world millions expressed their sympathies with the victims of the tragedy.

The post-9/11 era represents a reassertion of an acutely aggressive American state power both across global space (Smith 2005) and within domestic territory. If in the weeks following the events of 9/11 the moral boundaries that contained American identity behind a wall of indifferent nationalism dissolved somewhat amid the sympathetic global response, those walls went up again as the hawks in the Bush administration began to inch toward a global response. "Terrorism," Secretary of Defense Donald Rumsfeld agreed in response to a question from a reporter early on, "is not a country." In the face of a dispersed and largely invisible threat, the United States would respond with similar geographic agility.

To explain the new post-9/11 counterterrorism strategy to the American public, Bush, Rumsfeld, and other senior officials consistently used metaphors that rendered terrorism as deviantly natural. The purpose was to "drain the swamp": to transform the geographic milieu that allowed particular locations to become havens to terrorists. As Rumsfeld explained in another press conference:

> We'll have to deal with the networks. One of the ways to do that is to drain the swamp they live in. And that means dealing not only with the terrorists, but those who harbor terrorists (2001).

So if terrorism per se was not a country for Rumsfeld, networks such as al-Qaeda still had grounded geographies. As he said:

> The terrorists do not function in a vacuum. They don't live in Antarctica. They work, they train, and they plan in countries (2001).

The campaign to oust the Taliban from Afghanistan began in short order. B-52s dropped precision-guided bombs across the country, and special forces troops snagged possible al-Qaeda suspects, who were put on planes and shipped halfway around the world to the legal-geographic purgatory of Guantánamo Bay, Cuba.

And then there was Iraq. For the hawks in the administration, terrorism clearly *was* a country. Despite massive global opposition and the largest anti-American demonstrations since the 1960s, the Bush administration methodically and stubbornly marched toward a war that violated all of the principles of international law; a pre-emptive war based on what amounted to an unsupported rumor of a potential future threat. Among the only national politicians courageous enough to point out the utter insanity of the war, and indeed its moral contradiction, was conservative Texas Congressman Ron Paul, who said on the floor of the House of Representatives,

> We have for months now heard plenty of false arithmetic and lame excuses for why we must pursue a pre-emptive war of aggression against an impoverished third world nation 6,000 miles from our shores that doesn't even possess a navy or air force, on the pretense that it must be done for national security reasons. ... Military force is justified only in self-defense; naked aggression is the province of dictators and rogue states. This is the danger of a new "pre-emptive first strike" doctrine. America is the most moral nation on earth, founded on moral principles, and we must apply moral principles when deciding to use military force (2002).

The Mediated State and the Geopolitics of Scale

In all the criticism of the Bush administration's pre-emptive war against Iraq and its violation of all norms of international law, it is often forgotten that the Clinton administration sought to do roughly the same in 1998. For months, the administration lined up a similar string of arguments: about Saddam Hussein's open flouting of international authority as represented by the United Nations, about the need to enforce the rule of international law in the face of such defiance, and so forth. To put the final touches on the media campaign to prepare the nation for war, the administration staged a live town hall meeting at Ohio State University in February of 1998. The event was broadcast live on CNN to an estimated 200 million viewers worldwide, including, it seems, Hussein himself.

The event was designed to present the appearance of open public discussion that the name "town hall meeting" would suggest, an intimate forum for rational public debate about the benefits and costs of military confrontation. Yet the event was in fact heavily scripted. To attend, one needed a pass. Such passes, in turn, were divided between the roughly 1,000 red passes given to, as one critical account put it, "Ohio State University faculty, cadets, veterans and other military personnel, and local politicians," and the some 5,000 white passes made publicly available the day before. The format tightly regulated who could ask questions of the administration officials, restricting it to attendees with a red pass.

Despite all the precautions, the carefully managed spectacle was not quite carefully managed enough. A group of activists began chanting, "One, two, three four, we don't want your racist war!" and were disruptive enough that a producer agreed to allow one of them—Columbus-area substitute schoolteacher Jon Strange—to pose a question before the microphone in exchange for their silence. Stepping before the microphone, Strange asked a simple question of Secretary of State Madeleine Albright:

> Why bomb Iraq, when other countries have committed similar violations? ... Turkey has bombed Kurdish citizens. Saudi Arabia has tortured political and religious dissidents. Why does the U.S. apply different standards of justice to these countries (Albright, Cohen and Berger 1998)?

The ensuing exchange was as fascinating for what it revealed about the otherwise lack of vibrant debate in the contemporary

American public sphere as for what it revealed about the incoherence of Clinton administration geopolitical policy. Albright's response was both to note the administration's consistent condemnation of human rights abuses everywhere and to argue that Hussein was "qualitatively and quantitatively different from every brutal dictator that has appeared recently." There *was* something different about Iraq, she argued. Not willing to accept Albright's pat response, Strange continued:

> What do you have to say about dictators of countries like Indonesia, who we sell weapons to yet they are slaughtering people in East Timor? What do you have to say about Israel, who is slaughtering Palestinians, who impose martial law? What do you have to say about that? Those are our allies. Why do we sell weapons to these countries? Why do we support them? Why do we bomb Iraq when it commits similar problems (Albright, Cohen and Berger 1998)?

Albright quite obviously did not expect this sort of questioning and wilted a bit under the pressure, wondering aloud why critics of the administration were defending Hussein. Strange pressed on, retorting that the issue was not support for Hussein, but rather "that there needs to be consistent application of U.S. foreign policy." Frustrated with Albright's attempt to elude the question, he finally raised his voice and firmly said into the microphone, "You're not answering my question, Madame Albright!"

With that single exchange—broadcast live and in prime time—the entire war juggernaut was deflated in ways that mirrored the expression on Albright's face. I am not suggesting that a single question thwarted a war, but I am suggesting that the exchange made visible deep dissent over the move toward war with Iraq that limited the capacity of the administration to go to war. As Strange recounted of the surprising effectiveness of the protest,

> Though the town hall meeting was completely undemocratic and was arranged to silence dissent and promote the

> United States and its plan to bomb Iraq, it offered a ripe
> opportunity for protest. First of all, the presence of TV
> cameras probably kept security goons a little tame. I can't
> think of any other reason why they didn't just cart us off
> from the moment things got hectic, which is the standard
> practice. They just kept giving us more leeway. Secondly,
> the meeting was broadcast around the world LIVE. ...
> This meant that we weren't confined to a basketball arena
> in Ohio, but that we were able to tell the whole world that
> there are Americans who oppose the United States' war
> plans. (Albright, Cohen and Berger 1998)

The incident thus reflected a simultaneously mediated spectacle
and the concrete control of the media platform itself. In essence,
Strange and his colleagues had turned the scripted media stage
into a more fully public space and a protest platform. And, he
and his colleagues were convinced, the visibility of the encounter
had real effects:

> We left the town hall meeting convinced that our protests
> had been a success. The immediate effect we had on the
> national debate was evident in the national nightly news
> and in newspapers around the world the following day.
> We accomplished more than we could have ever imag-
> ined, with limited organization and limited resources. In
> 18 hours, we saw our ideas go from a small group of peo-
> ple talking at the community co-op to international TV
> (Albright, Cohen and Berger 1998).

The very fact that the administration felt it necessary to stage the
town hall meeting, and then to tightly control it, shows the
degree to which it understood the power of publicity.

The Power of Privacy

The second Bush administration, of course, took the scripting of
public spectacle to an entirely other level. Among the Bush

administration's strategies of managing the politics of dissent has been carefully managing its geography. The administration's strategic exploitation of a geography at once of publicity and of privacy—the careful centering of that which is consistent with the message, and the sequestering out of view of that which is not—played out at a variety of scales, in a variety of different spaces.

The management of domestic dissent has largely involved the public spaces of cities. During his first administration, Bush made important policy speeches before "public" audiences that were in fact carefully preselected. In an article in *The American Conservative*, James Bovard (2003) wrote with concern of the administration's application of Seattle-style "no-protest" zones to the provision of security for the president. Bovard recounts example after example in which the public spaces through which the president moves are swept clean of any visible hint of dissent:

> When Bush travels around the United States, the Secret Service visits the location ahead of time and orders local police to set up "free speech zones" or "protest zones" where people opposed to Bush policies (and sometimes sign-carrying supporters) are quarantined. These zones routinely succeed in keeping protesters out of presidential sight and outside the view of media covering the event.

This reflects, it seems, a broader movement to quite literally contain dissent; to locate it in bounded spaces more easily controlled.

The centrality of law—and the *geography* of law—to the conduct of state power and the dynamics of citizenship is clear with respect to a post-9/11 political landscape. In the same way that the *H. Rap Brown Act* was written in such broad and vague ways as to potentially make illegitimate and illegal a wide range of political actions in the 1960s, so too has law been deployed in aggressive ways to police dissent today (Cole and Dempsey 2002). New laws such as the *PATRIOT Act* restore such broad law enforcement latitude to the state that it prompts Don Mitchell to ask, "Is Civil

Disobedience a Form of Terrorism?" (2003b). The ACLU has concluded that "[t]he responses to dissent by many government officials … so clearly violate the letter and the spirit of the supreme law of the land, that they threaten the underpinnings of democracy itself"(American Civil Liberties Union 2003: 18).

Given the history of efforts to regulate dissent in the United States, there is reason to be concerned. Between the height of FBI power in the late 1960s and its involvement in the Wounded Knee occupation a few years later in 1973, the organization went through significant transformation, in which its previous power and autonomy waned significantly. Disclosure of the aggressive, sometimes illegal manner in which the FBI policed domestic political dissent led to reforms that limited the organization's power. In the wake of 9/11, however, then-Attorney General John Ashcroft worked aggressively not just to restore such power, but arguably to extend it. In the context of what was argued to be unprecedented threat, Ashcroft and others argued for similarly unprecedented powers to respond.

Particularly striking with respect to the geography of state power and politics of publicity is that Ashcroft's most controversial actions were perhaps best distinguished by their antigeography. Suspects and possible informants were held, for unknown reasons, in undisclosed locations, for indefinite length: In essence, they were "disappeared." What seems lost in much of what public discussion of these actions existed is that they were thoroughly legal—indeed, almost normal—under the statute written in the wake of the Oklahoma City bombing in 1995 (Sparke 1998). Under these laws, anti-immigrant racism was fused with domestic-security concerns to allow for the shockingly aggressive removal of the most basic rights held by American citizens (*Wall Street Journal* 2001) [16].

The deployment of American state power through the mechanism of privacy—in this case the obscuring from public view the practice of state power—played out in other spaces, too. In the diplomatic lead-up to the Iraq War, the administration exerted immense pressure on crucial United Nations member states to cobble together the so-called "coalition of the willing"; its strategies included covert espionage by British and American intelligence services against Security Council members as well as the Secretary General himself (*Observer* 2003). The purpose was to gain strategic insight that might allow them to better manage the diplomatic outcome, and with it the public legitimacy—and indeed the perceived international legality—of the war[17].

Politics in Other Spaces?

More broadly, the questions raised by these measures is not just whether a threat exists and for whom, but also how such threats are discursively and institutionally constituted, and to what degree the deployment of state power to counter them in the "public interest" is subject to the *public* visibility, accountability, and debate that are the hallmark of democratic practice.

My larger theoretical argument is that a more careful analysis of the politics of boundaries and scale, on one hand, and that of publicity and citizenship on the other, can provide richer insight into broader practices of democracy. We need, in short, to start thinking about somewhat counterintuitive ideas such as the geopolitics of home—about how larger geopolitical discourses and stakes can come together around the micro-spaces of the domestic home—or the way that states sometimes wield power by rendering their own practices as private, like those that take place behind the closed doors of a home.

Lynn Staeheli (1996) argues that it is a mistake both analytically and politically to assume that the public world of politics only ever takes place in public spaces and adds that there is a need to think through carefully exactly how distinctions between publicity and privacy are drawn in different contexts. Such a focus allows us to "identify spaces, interests, and actions that are more or less public without implying that either are *absolutely* or *ideally* public" (1996: 605). If it is the case that analysis of public dissent and scale can benefit from more nuanced appreciation of scale, it is equally true that work on scale can benefit from greater attention to the social construction of publicity. Put simply, who, what, and where is visible and public, and on what terms?

Even a theoretically and conceptually rich and sophisticated concept of boundaries can only ever be partial. As Kathleen Kirby (1996: 116) puts it, suggesting caution about uncritical views of boundaries and scale, "Recent world events suggest that on a geopolitical scale, as on the personal scale ..., boundaries may protect us as much as they confine us, or may protect even as they confine us." Continuing, she suggests that

> boundaries are often more than arbitrary: Their surfaces can contain, illustrate, and shield the existence of massive, tangible differences in intentions and interests that may emerge with murderous force when those limits are attenuated. Maintaining boundaries has seemed to many theorists a necessary element of political activity (1996: 66).

Although the process of "jumping scales" involves a particular aspect of social relations—dissolving the boundaries that define narrow notions of identity, perhaps—other boundaries must be simultaneously constructed or maintained. Whether this involves access to private spaces within which to organize a political protest, for instance, the securing of rights to protest in public space, or efforts to redraw legal boundaries, it is clear that geographies of scale are quite complex. The issue, then, is not only about expanding the scale of a given phenomenon—and therefore of dissolving boundaries—but of selectively dissolving and maintaining various kinds of boundaries and the spaces that they define.

The American Right learned this lesson a long time ago, crafting a well-oiled political machine that exhibits a quite effective politics of scale. Some on the Left have commented on the contrasting tactics of the Left and the Right. Kevin Mattson (2005), for example, suggests that perhaps the Left is too fixated on the 1960s as the model for progressive politics. "The Left is often identified as a series of marches," he writes, and "[p]rotest has become an easy way to express dissent." Instead, he suggests a need to learn from the success of the Right, which, he argues, employs a more disciplined set of strategies that largely eschews the theatrical politics of the streets for the more somber politics of organizing.

Yet it seems to me this perspective rather misses a crucial point. It ascribes a seamless coherence to both the tactics and the politics of the Right that belies the reality. The Right is not just business elites at fundraisers or intellectuals at Washington think tanks or radio talk show hosts projecting their words across the airwaves. The success of the Right is not only a function of its money and its intellectual capital, and of its careful exploitation of discourses of freedom and order in fora other than public demonstrations. It is also, as the 2004 election seems to have made clear, the preacher on a pulpit in small-town Ohio with a congregation willing to go out and do the political work to realize their vision of a just world. Likewise, it is the antiabortion activists who do more than write letters to editors, but engage in often quite aggressive—sometimes violent—disruptions of larger norms of public order.

Perhaps it is thus correct that the Left needs to *learn* from the past rather than borrow from it. The lesson, however, is perhaps not to throw the baby out with the proverbial bathwater; to leave the streets and the tactics of confrontational politics to the dustbins of history in favor of the more staid settings of legislative chambers and policy debates. Indeed, that suggests a perhaps too instrumental end to the business of protest politics, as if they were only ever about effecting a specific change, rather than also to do other kinds of work. The English word "demonstration" has become rather dead in its rote usage, but it is useful to consider its fundamental meaning. Like the Spanish word *manifestación*, the word points to the practice of making visible—in space—dissenting ways of thinking, being, and imagining the future. The function of such demonstrations or manifestations of dissent is often not only to speak before a larger public, but also at the same time to constitute what Nancy Fraser (1992) referred to as counter-publics.

Still, arguably the largest collective demonstrations in history failed to stop the juggernaut of the neoconservative war machine. And despite all of the failures of the subsequent war in Iraq—the missing weapons of mass destruction (WMD), the ongoing threat of civil war fragmenting the country into pieces, Abu-Ghraib, the some 18,000 estimated Iraqi and 1,500 American dead at the time I write this—the Right managed to re-elect President Bush with slim majorities of both the electoral and the popular votes, and to strengthen its dominance of the legislative branch. It remains to be seen what kinds of practices of dissent will be up to the task of providing real alternatives.

References

Abu-Lughod, L. (1990) The Romance of Resistance: Tracing Transformations of Power Through Bedouin Women, *American Ethnologist*, 17(1), pp. 41–55.

Acting Director FBI (1973a) teletype to U.S. Secret Service, In R. Dewing et al., *The FBI Files on the American Indian Movement and Wounded Knee.* Frederick, MD: University Publications of America, file number 105-203686-519.

—— (1973b) letter to Attorney General, In R. Dewing et al., *The FBI Files on the American Indian Movement and Wounded Knee.* Frederick, MD: University Publications of America, file number 105-203686-601.

—— (1973c) airtel to SAC Albany, In R. Dewing et al., *The FBI Files on the American Indian Movement and Wounded Knee.* Frederick, MD: University Publications of America, file number 100-462483-45.

—— (1973d) teletype to SACS, All and Post, SACS Wounded Knee Command, In R. Dewing et al., *The FBI Files on the American Indian Movement and Wounded Knee.* Frederick, MD: University Publications of America, file number 176-2404-257.

—— (1973e) teletype to All Offices and SAC Wounded Knee re: Disorders by American Indians in South Dakota, ARL, In R. Dewing et al., *The FBI Files on the American Indian Movement and Wounded Knee.* Frederick, MD: University Publications of America, file number 105-203686-693.

—— (1973f) memo to Joseph T. Sneed, In R. Dewing et al., *The FBI Files on the American Indian Movement and Wounded Knee*. Frederick, MD: University Publications of America, file number 176-2404-[unreadable].

Adams, P. C. (1996) Protest and the Scale Politics of Telecommunications, *Political Geography*, 15(5), pp. 419–441.

Albright, M., W. Cohen and S. Berger (1998) *Remarks at Town Hall Meeting, Ohio State University, Columbus, Ohio, February 18, 1998*, Washington, DC:U.S. Department of State, February 20, http://secretary.state.gov/www/statements/1998/980218.html [accessed on April 23, 2005].

Alter, J. (2000) Once More Unto the Breach, *Newsweek*, April 24(17), p. 38.

American Civil Liberties Union (2003) *Freedom Under Fire: Dissent in Post-9/11 America*. New York: ACLU, http://www.aclu.org.

Amnesty International (2001) *Canada: Amnesty International calls for public enquiry into alleged police brutality*, http://web.amnesty.org/library/Index/ENGAMR200032001 [accessed on January 29, 2005].

An act for preventing tumults and riotous assemblies, and for the more speedy and affectual punishing the rioters (1771) *Broadsides, leaflets, and pamphlets from America and Europe*, available from Printed Ephemera Collection; Portfolio 143, Folder 19, http://hdl.loc.gov/loc.rbc/rbpe.14301900 [accessed on March 6, 2004],

Anderson, B. (1983) *Imagined Communities: Reflections on the Origin and Spread of Nationalism*. London: Verso.

Anderson, R. et al. (Eds.) (1974) *Voices From Wounded Knee: In the Words of the Participants*. Rooseveltown, N.Y: Akwesasne Notes.

Anti-Riot Act (1968) 18 U.S.C., sections 2101, 2102 P.L. 90-284, April 11.

Assistant Attorney General (1973a) letter to Acting Director FBI re: Disorders at Wounded Knee, South Dakota, Caused by Members of the American Indian Movement, In R. Dewing et al., *The FBI Files on the American Indian Movement and Wounded Knee*. Frederick, MD: University Publications of America, file number 176-2404-306.

—— (1973b) memo to Acting Director FBI, In R. Dewing et al., *The FBI Files on the American Indian Movement and Wounded Knee*. Frederick, MD: University Publications of America, file number 176-2404-716.

Barber, B. R. (1992) Jihad vs. McWorld, *Atlantic Monthly*, March, pp. 53–63.

Bardach, A. L. (2002) *Cuba Confidential: Love and Vengeance in Miami and Havana*. New York: Random House.

Barnett, C. (2003) *Culture and Democracy: Media, Space, and Representation*. Tuscaloosa: University of Alabama Press.

Bates, R. F. (1973) memo to R. E. Gebhardt, In R. Dewing et al., *The FBI Files on the American Indian Movement and Wounded Knee*. Frederick, MD: University Publications of America, file number 176-2404-826.

Beatty, W. (1967) The Right to Dissent, *Congressional Record*, November 30, originally presented at West Virginia State Bar Meeting, October 19, 1967.

Bell, A. (2001) Public and Private Child: *Troxel v. Granville* and the Constitutional Rights of Family Members, *Harvard Civil Rights-Civil Liberties Law Review*, 36, p. 225.

Benjamin, W. (1978) *Reflections: Essays, Aphorisms, Autobiographical Writings*. New York: Shocken Books.

Blomley, N. (1994) *Law, Space, and the Geographies of Power*. New York: Guilford.

Bobiwash, R. (2003) Foreword, in *Under the Lens of the People: Our Account of the Peoples' Resistance to the FTAA, Québec City, April 2001*. Toronto: Peoples Lenses Collective.

Bovard, J. (2003) "Free-Speech Zone": The Administration Quarantines Dissent, *The American Conservative*, available from http://www.amconmag.com/12_15_03/feature.html [accessed on April 16, 2005].

Brecher, J. and T. Costello (1998) *Global Village or Global Pillage: Economic Reconstruction From the Bottom Up*. Cambridge, MA: South End Press.

Brown, D. (1971) *Bury My Heart at Wounded Knee: An Indian History of the American West*. New York: Holt, Rinehart.

Brown, H. R. (1969) *Die, Nigger, Die!* New York: Dial Press.

Brown, M. (1997) *RePlacing Citizenship: AIDS Activism and Radical Democracy*. New York: Guilford Press.

Byrd, R. (1967) Extremists in a Value-Vacuum, *Congressional Record*, November 30, pp. 34340–34342.

—— (2004) statement on Martin Luther King, In O. Bagwell and W. Walker, *Citizen King*. PBS American Experience, http://www.pbs.org/wgbh/amex/mlk/filmmore/pt.html.

Churchill, W. and J. Vander Wall (1988) *Agents of Repression: The FBI's Secret Wars Against the Black Panther Party and the American Indian Movement*. Boston: South End Press.

Cleaver, H. (1998) *The Zapatistas and the Electronic Fabric of Struggle*, In J. Holloway and E. Peláez (eds.), Zapatista! Reinventing Revolution in Mexico, London:Pluto Press, 1998.

Colburn, W. (1973) memo to Joseph T. Sneed, In R. Dewing et al., *The FBI Files on the American Indian Movement and Wounded Knee*. Frederick, MD: University Publications of America, file number 176-2404-787.

Cole, D. and J. X. Dempsey (2002) *Terrorism and the Constitution*. New York: The New Press.

Congressional Record (1967a) Creator of Insurrection, June 20.

—— (1967b) House Reads the Riot Act., July 21.

—— (1968) In Support of the Law and an Orderly Government, April 8.

Cooper, B. (2000) *INS Decision Memorandum in the Elian Gonzalez Case*. Washington: Department of Justice, http://uscis.gov/graphics/publicaffairs/elian.pdf [accessed on July 23, 2004].

Cramer, W. (1968) Federal Antiriot Law Needed to Deter Professional Rabble-Rousers, *Congressional Record*, January 18.

Cresswell, T. (2000) Falling Down: Resistance as Diagnostic, In J. P. Sharp et al. (Eds.), *Entanglements of Power: Geographies of Domination/Resistance.* London: Routledge, pp. 256–268.

De La Torre, M. A. (2003) *La Lucha for Cuba: Religion and Politics on the Streets of Miami.* Berkeley: University of California Press, p. 30.

Dellinger, D. (1975) *More Power than We Know: The People's Movement Toward Democracy.* Garden City, NY: Anchor Press/Doubleday.

Department of Justice (1973a) White Paper on Wounded Knee, In R. Dewing et al., *The FBI Files on the American Indian Movement and Wounded Knee.* Frederick, MD: University Publications of America.

—— (1973b) news release proposal, In R. Dewing et al., *The FBI Files on the American Indian Movement and Wounded Knee.* Frederick, MD: University Publications of America.

Dewing, R. (1995) *Wounded Knee II.* Freeman, SD: Pine Hill Press.

Drainville, A. (2002) Québec City 2001 and the Making of Transnational Subjects, *Socialist Register,* pp. 15–42.

Duncombe, S. (2002) Stepping Off the Sidewalk: Reclaim the Streets/NYC, In B. Shepard and R. Hayduk (Eds.), *From ACT UP to the WTO: Urban Protest and Community Building in the Era of Globalization.* New York: Verso, pp. 215–228.

The Economist (2001) All in the Familia, April 21.

Edwords, F. (2001) Chronicle of a Protest, *Humanist,* 61(4), p. 9.

Elliott, M. (1999) The New Radicals, *Newsweek,* December 13, pp. 36–39.

Epstein, J. (1970) *The Great Conspiracy Trial: An Essay on Law, Liberty and the Constitution.* New York: Random House.

Farber, D. (1988) *Chicago '68.* Chicago: The University of Chicago Press.

Federal Bureau of Investigation (1973) summary report, In R. Dewing et al., *The FBI Files on the American Indian Movement and Wounded Knee.* Frederick, MD: University Publications of America.

Felt, W. M. (1973a) letter to Acting Director FBI, In R. Dewing et al., *The FBI Files on the American Indian Movement and Wounded Knee.* Frederick, MD: University Publications of America, file number 176-2404-377.

—— (1973b) memo to R. E. Gebhardt re: Wounded Knee, In R. Dewing et al., *The FBI Files on the American Indian Movement and Wounded Knee.* Frederick, MD: University Publications of America, file number 176-2404-762.

—— (1973c) letter to Acting Director FBI re: Wounded Knee, In R. Dewing et al., *The FBI Files on the American Indian Movement and Wounded Knee.* Frederick, MD: University Publications of America, file number 176-2404-716.

—— (1979) *The FBI Pyramid From the Inside.* New York: G.P. Putnam's Sons.

Fishlow, D. (1973) Reading the Riot Act, *New Republic,* July 21, pp. 11–12.

Ford, R. (1999) Law's Territory: A History of Jurisdiction, *Michigan Law Review,* 97, p. 843.

Fraser, N. (1992) Rethinking the Public Sphere: A Contribution to the Critique of Actually Existing Democracy, In C. J. Calhoun (Ed.), *Habermas and the Public Sphere.* Cambridge, MA: MIT Press, pp. 109–142.

Garbus, M. (1974) General Haig of Wounded Knee, *Nation,* November 9, pp. 454–455.

Gebhardt, R. E. (1973a) memo to W. M. Felt, In R. Dewing et al., *The FBI Files on the American Indian Movement and Wounded Knee.* Frederick, MD: University Publications of America, file number 176-2404-23.

—— (1973b) memo to W. M. Felt re: Wounded Knee, In R. Dewing et al., *The FBI Files on the American Indian Movement and Wounded Knee.* Frederick, MD: University Publications of America, file number 176-2404-116.

Gilje, P. (1996) *Rioting in America.* Bloomington: Indiana University Press.

Glassman, J. F. (2002) From Seattle (and Ubon) to Bangkok: The Scales of Resistance to Corporate Globalization, *Environment and Planning D: Society and Space,* 20(5), pp. 513–533.

Goldberg, D. (2002) *The Racial State.* New York: Routledge.

González v. Reno et al. (2000) 212 F.3d 1338 (11th Cir.).

Grace, K. M. (2001) Québec City Prepares for Siege, *Newsmagazine,* 28(7), p. 13.

Griffen, G. E. (1965) *Anarchy, U.S.A.: In the Name of Civil Rights* (documentary film). American Media.

Habermas, J. (1989) *The Structural Transformation of the Public Sphere: An Inquiry into a Category of Bourgeois Society.* Cambridge, MA: MIT Press.

Hall, S. (1997) Old and New Identities, Old and New Ethnicities, In A. King (Ed.), *Culture, Globalization and the World-System.* Minneapolis: University of Minnesota Press, pp. 41–68.

Hanes, A. (2001) Border Battle: Some Mohawks of Akwesasne Want to Bring U.S. Protesters into Canada, *Montreal Gazette,* April 9, http://www.montrealgazette.com/summit/pages/010409/5058796.html [accessed April 20, 2001].

Headley, J. (1873) *The Great Riots of New York, 1712–873.* New York: E. B. Treat.

Hellstern, D. (1973) *Wounded Knee.* Washington: FBI Files on the American Indian Movement and Wounded Knee.

Herbert, S. (1997) *Policing Space: Territoriality and the Los Angeles Police Department.* Minneapolis: University of Minnesota Press.

Herod, A. (1991) The Production of Scale in the United States Labour Relations, *Area,* 23(1), pp. 82–88.

Hickey, N. (1973) Was the Truth Buried at Wounded Knee?, *TV Guide,* December 1, 8, 15, 22.

Hill, R. and R. Folgelson (1969) *A Study of Arrest Patterns in the 1960s Riots.* New York: Columbia University, Bureau of Applied Social Research.

Hoffman, A. S. (1973) memo to Director of the United States Information Agency.

Holder, E. (2000) statement of Deputy Attorney General Eric Holder, Jr. on the Arrival of Juan Miguel González. Department of Justice, http://www.usdoj.gov/opa/pr/2000/April/178dag.htm [accessed on July 23, 2004].

hooks, b. (1990) *Yearning: Race, Gender and Cultural Politics.* Boston: South End Press.

Hubbard, P. (2001) Sex Zones: Intimacy, Citizenship and Public Space, *Sexualities,* 4(1), pp. 51–71.

Isin, E. F. (2002) *Being Political: Geneologies of Citizenship.* Minneapolis: University of Minnesota Press.

Johnson, M. S. (1998) Gender, Race, and Rumours: Re-examining the 1943 Race Riots, *Gender & History,* 10(2), pp. 252–277.

Kinoy, A., H. E. Schwartz, and D. Peterson (1971) *Conspiracy on Appeal: Appellate Brief on Behalf of the Chicago Eight.* New York: Center for Constitutional Rights.

Kirby, K. (1996) *Indifferent Boundaries: Spatial Concepts of Human Subjectivity.* New York: The Guilford Press.

Krauthammer, C. (1999) Return of the Luddites, *Time,* December 13, p. 37.

Lefebvre, H. (2003 [1970]) *The Urban Revolution.* Minneapolis: University of Minnesota Press.

Leroux, D. (2001a) Next Stop: Québec City, *Canadian Dimension,* 35(2), p. 20.

—— (2001b) Québec City: 'Free-Trade' Flashpoint, *Dollars & Sense,* March/April (234), p. 31.

—— (2001c) Will Canadian border close to FTAA protesters? *Straight Goods,* available from http://www.straightgoods.com/FTAA/010409Leroux.shtml [accessed on January 29, 2005].

Levine, R. (2000) *Cuban Miami.* New Brunswick, NJ: Rutgers University Press.

Lyman, S. (1991) *Wounded Knee 1973: A Personal Account.* Lincoln: University of Nebraska Press.

Mann, J. (1992) Deep Throat: An Institutional Analysis, *The Atlantic Monthly,* May 269(5), pp. 106–112, available from http://www.theatlantic.com/issues/92may/9205deepthroat.htm [accessed on November 23, 2000].

Marston, S. (2004) Space, Culture, State: Uneven Developments in Political Geography, *Political Geography,* 23, pp. 1–16.

Martin, D. and B. Miller (2003) Space and Contentious Politics, *Mobilization,* 8(2), pp. 143–156.

Massey, D. (1994) *Space, Place, and Gender.* Minneapolis: University of Minnesota Press.

Mattson, K. (2005) Goodbye to All That, *American Prospect,* available from http://www.prospect.org/web/page.ww?section=root&name=ViewWeb&articleId=9389 [accessed on April 5, 2005].

McAdam, D., S. Tarrow, and C. Tilly (2001) *Dynamics of Contention.* Cambridge: Cambridge University Press.

McElravy, E. (2001) Enemies of Trade, *Reason,* 33(3), p. 36.

Means, R. and M. Wolf (1995) *Where White Men Fear to Tread: The Autobiography of Russell Means.* New York: St. Martin's Press.

Meet the Press (2000) NBC, April 23.

Meissner, D. (2000) *INS Decision in the Elián González Case.* United States Immigration and Naturalization Service, http://uscis.gov/graphics/publicaffairs/statements/Elian.htm [accessed on July 22, 2004].

The Miami Herald (1999a) Clinton Appeals that Politics Not Intrude on the Plight of Cuban Boy, December 18, accessed online from Newspaper Source database, July 23, 2004.

—— (1999b) Castro Demands U.S. Return Rescued 5-year-old Boy, December 5, accessed online from Newspaper Source database, July 23, 2004.

—— (1999c) Tensions Escalating between U.S., Cuba over 6-year-old Boy, December 6, accessed online from Newspaper Source database, July 23, 2004.

—— (2000a) Cuban Boy's Plight Provides Political Fodder for Presidential Campaign, January 9, accessed online from Newspaper Source database, July 23, 2004.

—— (2000b) Hundreds Rally in Miami to Protest Repatriation of Haitian Migrants, January 2, accessed online from Newspaper Source database, July 23, 2004.

—— (2000c) Protests Have Dose of Choreography Driven in Large Part by the Presence of TV, January 9, accessed online from Newspaper Source database, July 23, 2004.

—— (2000d) Crowd of Protesters Swells from Hundreds to Thousands, April 13, accessed online from Newspaper Source database, July 23, 2004.

—— (2000e) Elián's Relatives Have Lost All Semblance of Normalcy in Their Private Lives, January 9, accessed online from Newspaper Source database, July 23, 2004.

—— (2000f) Video Shows Elián Telling Father He Doesn't Want to go Back to Cuba, April 13, accessed online from Newspaper Source database, July 23, 2004.

—— (2000g) Were Guns and Riot Gear Necessary to Grab a Child in the Dawn? April 22, accessed online from Newspaper Source database, July 23, 2004.

—— (2000h) Polls Show Americans Remain Divided Over Elián Seizure, April 24, accessed online from Newspaper Source database, July 23, 2004.

Miller, B. (2000) *Geography and Social Movements: Comparing Antinuclear Activism in the Boston Area.* Minneapolis: University of Minnesota Press.

Mitchell, D. (1995) The End of Public Space? People's Park, Definitions of the Public, and Democracy, *Annals of the Association of American Geographers,* 85, pp. 109–133.

—— (1996) Political Violence, Order, and the Legal Construction of Public Space: Power and the Public Forum Doctrine, *Urban Geography,* 17, pp. 152–178.

—— (2003a) *The Right to the City: Social Justice and the Fight for Public Space.* New York: Guilford Press.

—— (2003b) Is Civil Disobedience a Form of Terrorism? *Perspectives: Syracuse University Magazine,* 20(1), p. 19.

Mitchell, D. and L. Staeheli (2004) Permitting Protest: Constructing—and Dismantling—the Geography of Dissent in the United States, Annual Meeting of the Association of American Geographers, Philadelphia.

Mitchell v. Canada (Minister of National Revenue) (1997) (5266 (F.C.)), available from http://www.canlii.org/ca/cas/fct/1997/1997fct10457.html [accessed on February 9, 2005].

Monkkonen, E. (1981) A Disorderly People? Urban Order in the Nineteenth and Twentieth Centuries, *Journal of American History,* 68(3), pp. 539–559.

Montreal Gazette (2001) Border Battle: Some Mohawks of Akwesasne Want to Bring U.S. Protesters into Canada, April 9, available from http://www.montrealgazette.com/summit/pages/010409/5058796.html [accessed on April 20, 2001].

National Advisory Commission on Civil Disorders (1968) *Report of the National Advisory Commission on Civil Disorders.* New York: E.P. Dutton & Co., Inc.

National Committee Against Repressive Legislation (1973) *The 'Antiriot' Law: Weapon Against Dissent.* Pamphlet. Folder: National Conspiracy Suit; Class Action Challenging the 1968 Anti-Riot Act, 1973, box 65, Wounded Knee Legal Defense/Offense Committee Records, Minnesota State Historical Society, St. Paul, Minnesota.

Newsweek (1967a) An American Tragedy, 1967—Detroit, August 7, pp. 18–22.

—— (1967b) Newark Boils Over, July 24, pp. 21–22.

—— (1973) Guerrilla Theater, April 9, p. 38.

—— (2000a) The Elián Endgame, April 10(15), p. 27.

—— (2000b) The End of Innocence, April 24(17), p. 34.

—— (2000c) Cashing In on Little Elián, May 8(19), p. 32.

—— (2001) Perspectives, April 30(18).

New York Times (1973) Dispute over Indian Burial Worsens at Wounded Knee, April 30.

—— (1975) Army Tested Secret Civil Disturbance Plan at Wounded Knee, Memos Show, p. 32.

Obregón Pagán, E. (2000) Los Angeles Geopolitics and the Zoot Suit Riots, 1943, *Social Science History,* 24(1), pp. 223–256.

Observer (2003) Revealed: US dirty tricks to win vote on Iraq war, March 2, available from http://observer.guardian.co.uk/iraq/story/0,12239,905936,00.html [accessed on March 3, 2003].

O'Connor, A. (2003) Punk Subculture in Mexico and the Antiglobalization Movement: A Report from the Front, *New Political Science,* 25(1), pp. 42–53.

O'Connor, T. (1967) North Meets the Outsider, *Congressional Record,* August 3.

Oglala Sioux Tribal Council (1973) court order, March 16.

Olkon, S., G. Epstein Nieves, and M. Merzer (2000) Cuban Exiles Stage Traffic-Disrupting Protests in Miami, *Miami Herald,* accessed online from Newspaper Source database, July 23, 2004.

O'Reilly, K. (1989) *Racial Matters: The FBI's Files on Black America, 1960–1972.* New York: The Free Press.

Patterson, B. (1988) *The Ring of Power: The White House Staff and Its Expanding Role in Government.* New York: Basic Books, Inc.

Paul, R. (2002) *Arguments Against a War in Iraq,* http://www.house.gov/paul/congrec/congrec2002/cr090402.htm [accessed on April 12, 2005].

Portland (1973) teletype to Acting Director FBI, In R. Dewing et al., *The FBI Files on the American Indian Movement and Wounded Knee.* Frederick, MD: University Publications of America, file number 176-2404-[unknown].

Potter, C. B. (1998) *War on Crime: Bandits, G-Men, and the Politics of Mass Culture.* New Brunswick, NJ: Rutgers University Press.

Remington, S. (1973) statement to the Press regarding *Burgwin et al. v. Mattson et al.,* In *Wounded Knee Legal Defense/Offense Committee Records.* St. Paul: Minnesota State Historical Society, Box 65.

Reno, J. (2000) *Statement.* Washington: United States Department of Justice.

Richmond, B. (1973) letter to Wounded Knee Defense/Offense Committee, *Wounded Knee Legal Defense/Offense Committee Records,* St. Paul: Minnesota State Historical Society, Box 65.

Rieff, D. (1987) *Going to Miami.* New York: Simon & Schuster.

Ross, J. (2000) *The War against Oblivion: The Zapatista Chronicles.* Monroe, ME: Common Courage Press.

Routledge, P. (1994) Backstreets, Barricades, and Blackouts: Urban Terrains of Resistance in Nepal, *Environment and Planning D: Society and Space,* 12(5), pp. 559–578.

—— (1998) Going Globile: Spatiality, Embodiment, and Media-tion in the Zapatista Insurgency, In G. Ó Tuathail and S. Dalby (Eds.), *Rethinking Geopolitics.* New York: Routledge, pp. 240–60.

—— (2000) 'Our Resistance Will Be as Transnational as Capital,' *Geo Journal,* (52), pp. 25–33.

—— (2003) Convergence Space: Process Geographies of Grassroots Globalization Networks, *Transactions of the Institute of British Geographers,* (28), pp. 333–349.

Ruddick, S. (1996) Constructing Difference in Public Spaces: Race, Class, and Gender as Interlocking Systems, *Urban Geography,* 17(2), pp. 132–151.

Rudé, G. (1959) The London "Mob" of the Eighteenth Century, *The Historical Journal,* 2(1), pp. 1–18.

Rumsfeld, D. (2001) *DoD News Briefing—Secretary Rumsfeld.* Washington: Department of Defense, http://www.defenselink.mil/transcripts/2001/t09182001_t0918sda.html [accessed on April 12, 2005].

SAC Minneapolis (1973) teletype to Acting Director FBI, In R. Dewing et al., *The FBI Files on the American Indian Movement and Wounded Knee.* Frederick, MD: University Publications of America, file number 176-2404-90.

SAC San Francisco (1973) airtel to Director FBI, In R. Dewing et al., *The FBI Files on the American Indian Movement and Wounded Knee.* Frederick, MD: University Publications of America, file number 176-2404-1403.

Schieffer, B. (2001) Commentary, *Face the Nation,* CBS, April 22.

Sharp, J. et al. (Eds.) (2000) *Entanglements of Power: Geographies of Domination/Resistance.* London: Routledge.

Sibley, D. (1995) *Geographies of Exclusion: Society and Difference in the West.* London: Routledge.

Situationists International (1965) *The Decline and Fall of the Spectacle-Commodity Economy,* http://www.bopsecrets.org/1965WattsRiot.html [accessed on May 24, 2004].

Smith, D. (1973) The Media Coup D'Etat, *The Nation,* June 25, pp. 806–809.

Smith, N. (1992) Contours of a Spatialized Politics: Homeless Vehicles and the Production of Geographical Scale, *Social Text,* (33), pp. 54–81.

—— (2005) *The Endgame of Globalization.* New York: Routledge.

Smith, P. and R. Warrior (1996) *Like a Hurricane: The Indian Movement from Alcatraz to Wounded Knee.* New York: New Press.

Smith, S. (1989) Society, Space and Citizenship: Human Geography After the New Right, *Transactions of the Institute of British Geographers New Series,* (14), pp. 144–156.

Smith, T. (2001) Protests Against the Summit of the Americas Take Place All Over the U.S., *CBS News,* April 21.

Sneed, J. T. (1973) memo to Acting Director FBI, In R. Dewing et al., *The FBI Files on the American Indian Movement and Wounded Knee.* Frederick, MD: University Publications of America, file number 176-2404-[unreadable].

Sparke, M. (1998) Outsides Inside Patriotism: The Oklahoma Bombing and the Displacement of Heartland Geopolitics, In G. Ó Tuathail and S. Dalby (Eds.), *Rethinking Geopolitics.* New York: Routledge, pp. 198–223.

St. Louis (1973) teletype to Acting Director FBI, In R. Dewing et al., *The FBI Files on the American Indian Movement and Wounded Knee.* Frederick, MD: University Publications of America, file number 176-2404-331.

Staeheli, L. (1996) Publicity, Privacy, and Women's Political Action, *Environment and Planning D: Society and Space,* 14, pp. 601–619.

The Toronto Star (2000) View from Quebec a Feeding Frenzy of Alarm, September 2, accessed from online database.

This Week (2000) ABC, April 23.

Thompson, E. P. (1971) Moral Economy of the English Crowd in the Eighteenth Century, *Past and Present,* (50), pp. 76–136.

Time (1973a) Birth of a Nation, March 26, p. 22.

—— (1973b) A Suspenseful Show of Red Power, March 19, pp. 16–18.

—— (1973c) Raid at Wounded Knee, March 12, p. 21.

—— (1999) War over a Poster Boy, December 13 (24), p. 68.

—— (2000a) A Big Battle for a Little Boy, January 17(2), p. 58.

—— (2000b) "I Love My Child," April 17(15), p. 24.

—— (2000c) What Can a Kid Decide? May 11(18), p. 32.

—— (2000d) Reno's Showdown, April 24(16), p. 32.

—— (2000e) The Elián Grab, May 11(18), pp. 24.

Tremblay v. Québec (Attorney General) (2001) (J.Q. No. 1504) (Translation from original French).

U.S. News & World Report (1968) Insurrection: Outlook in U.S., April 29, pp. 38–41.

—— (2000) Who Speaks for Elián?, May 11(17), p. 21.

U.S. Senate (1967a) *Antiriot Bill Hearings, Part 1.* Washington: U.S. Government Printing Office.

—— (1967b) *Report on Interference with Civil Rights.* Washington: U.S. Government Printing Office.

U.S. Senate Select Committee to Study Governmental Operations with Respect to Intelligence Activities (1976) *Final Report—Book 3, Supplementary Detailed Staff Reports on Intelligence Activities and the Rights of Americans.* Washington: U.S. Government Printing Office.

United States v. Dennis Banks (1974) trial transcript, Volume 84; copy available in *Wounded Knee Legal Defense/Offense Committee Records,* St. Paul: Minnesota State Historical Society.

Wall Street Journal (2001) White House Seeks to Remove Time Limit on Surveillance Part of Antiterrorism Bill, October 5, p. A16.

Washington Post (2002) Looking for Elian: What Happened to the Little Boy Whose Life Was Set Adrift?, March 10, available from http://www.washingtonpost.com/ac2/wp-dyn?pagename=article&contentId=A60888-2002Mar&&notFound=true [accessed on July 17, 2004].

Will, G. F. (2000) Compassionate Liberalism, *Newsweek,* May 11(18), p. 80.

Wilson, D., L. Eagle Bull, and E. Nelson (1973) letter to H. Wood and M. Franklin, In R. Dewing et al., *The FBI Files on the American Indian Movement and Wounded Knee.* Frederick, MD: University Publications of America, file number 176-2404-252.

World Trade Organization (2005) *WTO,* http://www.wto.org [accessed on January 20, 2005].

Wounded Knee Information and Defense Fund (1973) information letter, *Wounded Knee Legal Defense/Offense Committee Records,* St. Paul: Minnesota State Historical Society, Box 99.

Wounded Knee Legal Defense/Offense Committee, (1973) Wounded Knee Legal Defense/Offense Committee Formed, In R. Dewing et al., *The FBI Files on the American Indian Movement and Wounded Knee.* Frederick, MD: University Publications of America.

Wounded Knee Legal Defense/Offense Committee Records (1973) Fellow Oglalas and Fellow Patriots, available from Box 23, Folder 21, file number 151 K 3 8F.

Zakaria, F. (1999) After the Storm Passes, *Newsweek,* December 13, p. 40.

—— (2001) The New Fact of the Left, *Newsweek,* April 30, p. 32.

Zimmerman, B. (1976) *Airlift to Wounded Knee.* Chicago: Swallow Press.

Zwarenstein, C. (2001) Opening the Border for FTAA, *Eye Weekly,* April 21, available from http://www.eye.net/eye/issue/issue_03.15.01/news/ftaa.html [accessed on January 29, 2005].

Notes

1. Steve Herbert's work on policing is an exception to some extent, though his focus is rather more broad than simply the policing of dissent in public space (1997).
2. The association between visibility, identity, and political legitimacy occurs beyond riots. Mexican military officials, for example, commented on the anonymity of masked *campesinos* who could not be otherwise clearly marked as Zapatistas, and thus as threats to the state.
3. In truth, my theoretical argument would be a broader one than the historical aspect of it. It seems to me the argument I present here could be usefully deployed—or at least tested—in vastly different historical contexts. This is not to say there is not something new about contemporary protest, of course, but rather that there is a tendency sometimes to both exaggerate the differences of contemporary protest and with it to leave out critical analysis of the changing nature of protest politics.
4. In its 1968 "interview with an authority on riots," for example, *U.S. News & World Report* sought, "in the wake of the riots that rocked cities across the nation," answers to two basic questions: "Is full-scale insurrection next on the schedule, [and] what is being done to meet the threat?" (*U.S. News & World Report* 1968: 38).
5. As Claire Potter (1998) explains, the federalization of police authority came in part as a response to new criminal threats. The kind of public bandits the FBI was initially designed, in part, to apprehend—the auto bandits that freely crossed state lines and, thus, necessitated an equally

189

mobile police force—were themselves enabled by that same state. Aside from the road network established by the federal state that allowed relatively cheap and privatized mobility—both important to this new sort of crime—criminality itself was bound up in complex state transformations. "[T]he elevation of bandits to a politicized folk status," she argues, "can be linked to the history of . . . state concentration, capital concentration, and the proletarianization of labor . . . [p]recisely because they articulate a prenational past . . . [and] reject modern, state-centered political solutions"(Potter 1998: 84–85).

6. Susan Smith observed a similar discourse of citizenship articulated by the "New Right" in the 1980s (1989).

7. The *Antiriot Act* was also known as the *Stokeley Carmichael Act*.

8. Indeed, the grand jury that indicted the Chicago Eight also considered indicting the media networks as well.

9. The Watergate scandal broke during Wounded Knee. According to Mann (1992), the famous "Deep Throat" source who leaked details of the illegal break-in at the hotel to journalist Bob Woodward was almost certainly a highly placed FBI official. Particularly likely, in his view, were three men involved in FBI decision-making at Wounded Knee: Mark Felt, Charles Bates, and Gray himself. In 2005, press reports confirmed that the source was in fact Felt. As Mann explained, the possibility that an FBI official brought down a president is interesting for what it illuminates about the internal dynamics of the state. The FBI was in a period of transition following Hoover's death in 1972. During this period the Nixon White House sought to bring the historically autonomous organization under closer control. The appointment of Gray from the Attorney General's office to the Acting Directorship of the FBI was one symptom, but the tensions expressed at Wounded Knee were likely connected to these larger issues as well.

10. AIM's version of events was just the opposite: that the FBI helicopter had fired indiscriminately on people who had gone to collect the bundles.

11. Warner's plan itself was highly secret. "Information about the battle plan," one FBI memo noted, "was on a need-to-know basis" (Bates 1973). The plan was so sensitive, in fact, that neither the Pentagon nor the Attorney General's office were willing to provide a copy to the FBI.

12. One might speculate that the leak was quite deliberately intended to put pressure on the occupiers to peacefully end the occupation. As with earlier Army plans, however, the FBI was not informed of its details. Referencing the *New York Times* article, one senior FBI official explained, "The information which we in the FBI sought officially now appears in the national media. This would indicate a leak or the information was furnished to the news media, but denied to the" (Bates 1973). This senior official was clearly unhappy with this. As he explained in another memo,

"It is inconceivable that the foremost law enforcement agency, would not be given a copy of a plan of operation in which it is both directly and indirectly involved" (Bates 1973). He further expressed the view that while the FBI might not be involved directly in the assault, "this does not preclude the possibility that if something goes wrong the FBI will be immediately dispatched to remedy a bad situation, as has been done in the past."

13. *La Lucha* is a term rooted in the Cuban independence movement.

14. Only later—after the child was reunited with his father—did a psychologist who examined the boy indicate that the attachment Elián had to his cousin was less that of a son to a mother, than a schoolboy crush.

15. Post-Seattle, security officials were much more prepared to ensure their control over city public spaces. The Commander of Washington, D.C., Metro Police, for example, reported he had personally visited Seattle, Prague, and a variety of other sites of significant protest events with the explicit intent of learning about the evolution of protest tactics (Mitchell and Staeheli 2004).

16. As in the past, the political logic behind these new laws and their aggressive enforcement is also a geographic logic. The new "Department of "Homeland Defense" guards the defenseless American public against the terrorist lurking amid small towns and suburbs.

17. The targets of the espionage—Chile, Pakistan, Guinea, Angola, Cameroon, and Bulgaria—were of particular concern to American and British officials because of their lukewarm support for the war and their active efforts to avert it through diplomatic means.

Index